Horse Rider's Mechanic

Workbook 2:

Your Balance

Jane Myers

Equiculture Publishing

Edition 1

Copyright © July 2014

ISBN 978-0994156112

Email: stuart@equiculture.com.au

Disclaimer

The author and publisher shall have neither liability nor responsibility to any person or entity with respect to any loss or damage or injury caused or alleged to be caused directly or indirectly by the information contained in this book. While the book is as accurate as the author can make it, there may be errors, omissions and inaccuracies.

About this book

Without good balance, you cannot ride to the best of your ability. After improving your position (the subject of the first book in this series), improving your balance will lead to you becoming a more secure and therefore confident rider. Improving your balance is the key to *further* improving your riding. Most riders need help with this area of their riding life, yet it is not a commonly taught subject.

This book contains several lessons for each of the three paces, walk, trot and canter. It builds on **Horse Rider's Mechanic Workbook 1: Your Position**, teaching you how to implement your now improved position and become a safer and more secure rider. The lessons allow you to improve at your own pace, in your own time. They will compliment any instruction you are currently receiving because they concentrate on issues that are generally not covered by most instructors.

This book also provides instructors, riding coaches and trainers with lots of valuable tips for teaching clients how to improve their balance. You cannot afford to miss out on this great opportunity to learn!

Thank you for buying this book and please consider either leaving a review or contacting us with feedback, stuart@equiculture.com.au

About the author

I (Jane Myers) AKA **The Horse Rider's Mechanic**, teach the subject of Rider Biomechanics. Rider Biomechanics is the subject of what your body is meant to be doing when riding, and if it isn't, how you can fix it. It focuses on the rider in particular, the idea being that until you sort out your rider problems (i.e. your position and balance), you cannot expect to ride correctly and therefore you cannot expect your horse to go correctly.

I have an MSc in Equine Science and I am the author of several professional books about horses. I have lived and breathed horses from a young age and consider myself to be very fortunate in that I have been able to spend my life life riding, training and studying these amazing animals.

Along with Stuart Myers (my best friend and husband) I have a business called Equiculture. We are particularly interested in sustainable horsekeeping practices and issues, such as low stress horse management that also delivers environmental benefits. We present workshops to horse owners in Australia, the USA and the UK about sustainable horse and horse property management.

See the Equiculture website www.equiculture.com.au where you will find lots of great information about horsekeeping and please join the mailing list while you are there!

We also have another website that supports the Horse Rider's Mechanic series of workbooks. This website is www.horseridersmechanic.com why not have a look?

Photo credits

All photos and diagrams by Jane Myers and Stuart Myers unless otherwise accredited. Any errors and omissions please let us know.

Contents

By reading this book you will…

Improve performance

You and your horse will work better together. You will improve your position, balance and application of the aids. This will give your horse a better understanding of what he or she is meant to do and you will both be able to perform better (whatever you do together). A never ending upwards spiral!

Increase your safety and security

Riding is classed as one of the more dangerous sports and pastimes. In particular the position and balance of a rider are inextricably linked. In turn they determine how safe and secure a rider is. With the help of these books you will now be able to give yourself a whole body 'tune up' and your safety and security will improve greatly because of it. Think of it as putting your body through a thorough check up followed by making adjustments based on what you have found.

Enjoy your riding more

Becoming a better rider will lead to more enjoyment as you experience 'light bulb moments' over and over again. Learning is fun as you just keep getting better. Your horse will move more freely as he or she learns that you are becoming easier to carry. A comfortable horse that is not stressed is more fun (and safer) to ride.

Save money

Improving your riding takes time, patience and money. It is a very apt saying that if you look after the basics (the foundations) then what follows will look after itself. The *Horse Rider's Mechanic* series of workbooks focuses on the foundations. Without good solid foundations, nothing substantial can be built.

Riding is an expensive sport or pastime. We are not saying you should cut corners however these books will help you to progress in such a way that any instruction that you do have will be more cost effective because you will have better foundations.

Reduce or eliminate stress for your horse

A rider has the potential to inflict a huge amount of stress on a horse – in so many ways. At Equiculture we teach people how to minimise or eliminate that stress. Our main website **www.equiculture.com.au** deals with the horse management side of stress reduction. This series of books (and the Horse Rider's Mechanic website that supports them, **www.horseridersmechanic.com**) are about how you can reduce or eliminate that stress when riding.

So much is discussed and written about how important it is for a horse to be 'straight', 'supple', 'balanced' and 'relaxed'. This series of books teaches you how to make sure that you uphold your part of the bargain - by working to be the best rider you can be.

Whatever your riding interests, whether you ride just for fun or to compete (or both), it is important that you ride to the best of your ability.

A rider's responsibilities

As a horse owner/rider you should ensure that your horse is free from stress and pain.

A domestic horse should be kept in such a way that does not cause stress. Any horse that is being used for riding should be fit, strong and well enough for the purpose. The horse should be trained enough so that he or she is capable of performing the required task. The horse should be fed correctly, have correct hoof care, teeth care, skin care etc. All gear that is used on the horse (for riding or handling) should fit correctly and should not inflict pain.

All of these subjects and more are covered by articles and books on the Horse Rider's Mechanic website www.horseridersmechanic.com and on our other website www.equiculture.com.au

A rider should aim to improve their position and balance and method of signalling ('aids') so that the horse finds it as easy as possible to carry the rider and understands what he or she is being asked to do. A rider should aim to keep learning so that they can continue to improve their horse management and rider skills.

Support

Remember, there are many articles on **www.horseridersmechanic.com** that support the information in this book. It is up to you whether you read them first or read them as they are referred to in the text. They include subjects such as *Your safety, Your confidence, Your horse, Your horse's gear, Your body, Your riding area* and *Your assistant*. There are many others listed on the same page that you should find interesting.

In addition: if there is anything you do not understand or need help with after reading this book (or the others in this series) post a question on the Horse Rider's Mechanic Facebook page:

www.facebook.com/horseridersmechanic

This Facebook page is especially for the readers of these books. Help is at hand!

You may never have come across this kind of information before (at least not in the way it is presented in the Horse Rider's Mechanic series of books) so I hope you enjoy this new 'journey' that you are about to take as have indeed so many of my clients in the past!

A further disclaimer

Just to remind you, I am *not* a human body worker (physiotherapist etc.) but a horse riding instructor that specialises in dealing with horse rider position and balance issues. Therefore I am very interested in human biomechanics and I talk/write extensively on this subject, but this does not make me a doctor or any other type of human health expert. Make sure you have any real problems with your body checked out by a professional (i.e. a physiotherapist etc).

How to get the most from this book

Now we will look at your balance in detail. The information in the following sections is thorough but if you simply read the rest of this book and then attempt to make changes from what you remember you may miss some very important points.

I suggest you do the following to maximise your chances of succeeding in your quest to improve your riding:

- Start by reading through the rest of this book *at least* once. As you go through it identify your own particular problems. You could write out a few notes on some pieces of card for example.
- On these pieces of card write out the outline of one lesson at a time and take it with you next time you ride.
- If you are working through this book with an assistant they can read the lessons out to you while you ride. They can also describe what they see

to you, so finding someone who will help you is great if this is possible (see the **Horse Rider's Mechanic website article *Your assistant***).

- The main information that you need to complete the lesson is dot pointed under the heading in each lesson that starts ***Learning***...
- At the end of every lesson there is a section that starts ***You are ready to move on to the next lesson when***... Make sure you do not move on to the next lesson until you have accomplished what is described in that section.
- For some people the whole process may only take little time, for others much longer. *However long it takes, take your time*. You will be surprised at what you learn about your riding by being so thorough.
- A common instruction that I have given while you are working through the various lessons is to *experiment* with different amounts of muscle tension, weighting etc. in each part of your body. Good riding involves achieving the right amount of muscle tension in each area of the body, not too little and not too much. By increasing tension and then decreasing it you should find what is correct for you. You can only learn this through 'trial and error'. Only you can experiment and learn what your body needs by making an area more 'still' or make an area more 'loose' and noticing if this improves your riding or not.
- Once you have worked your way through the lessons start at the beginning and work through them again, *at least one more time*. This is important because as you make adjustments to some parts of your body, other areas may try to compensate and you may end up 'undoing' an area that you previously corrected. As you learn to be more intuitive about your body as a rider you will be able to make minor adjustments quite easily in time, but at first you will need to apply quite a bit of concentration to do this.

- Don't attempt to 'school' your horse at the same time you are doing these lessons as this will prevent you from concentrating properly on the various feelings that you need for feedback. This feedback will give you the information that you need to make any necessary changes. For these sessions your horse is simply helping you to improve as a rider which in turn will benefit your horse enormously in the future.

Remember: it is a good idea to read through the articles on www.horseridersmechanic.com. These articles will prepare you for the instructions in this book. Have a look at the Horse Rider's Mechanic Facebook page: www.facebook.com/horseridersmechanic

You can post any questions that you have as you work through this book and the others in this series. Here we go!

The gaits

Even if you are an experienced rider please do not be tempted to skip this section about the gaits as you may miss a 'light bulb moment'.

Firstly it may be helpful for you to understand a couple of terms from the science of 'gait analysis', which is the study of human and animal movement.

A 'stride' is a complete cycle of a limb's function. It starts as a foot touches down and ends when the foot is about to touch down again. A stride is separated into two phases, the 'swing phase' and the 'stance phase'.

The swing phase is when the limb is swinging forward through the air, the stance phase is when the limb is in contact with the ground and the body is moving forwards over the top of that limb.

The right hind and the left fore are in the 'swing phase' because they are moving through the air... and the left hind and the right fore are in the 'stance phase' because they are in contact with the ground.

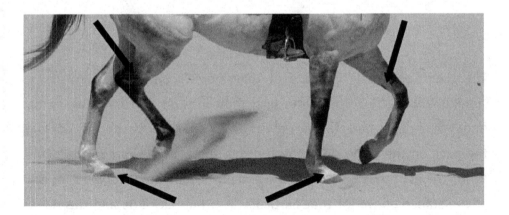

Walk

The walk is a **four beat gait**. While riding a walking horse you can hear the hoof beats *one, two, three, four, one, two, three, four...* This is because in the walk the four hooves of the horse touch down at separate, evenly spaced times. Starting with a hind hoof, then the fore on the same side, then the other hind followed by the fore on that side.

There is no **period of suspension** in the walk as there is in the trot and canter (suspension means when all four hooves are off the ground). This makes the walk the easiest gait to ride in terms of position and balance for the rider.

The footfalls of walk

In walk a hind hoof lands first, closely followed by the fore hoof on the same side. Then the hind hoof on the other side, closely followed by the fore hoof on that side. There is no period of suspension in the walk.

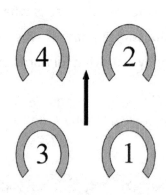

The rider feels first one side of their horse's back dip, then lift, as simultaneously the other side dips, then lifts. As the hind leg swings under the horse's body (as part of the swing phase for that particular leg), the back on the same side dips and the rider's hip lowers on that side. When the hoof touches the ground and pushes the horse forward (as part of the stance phase for that particular leg) the back lifts and the rider's hip on that side lifts simultaneously. This is covered in detail in the section **Riding the walk**.

It is a *symmetrical* gait (like trot, but unlike canter) because the horse carries out symmetrical actions with both sides of their body.

In this picture the left hind has swung forward and is in contact with the ground (it is starting the stance phase) the left fore is about to touch down (so it is at the very end of the swing phase and about to also start the stance phase). The right hind has finished the stance phase and is starting the swing phase and the right fore is still in the stance phase.

In this picture the left hind is starting the swing phase, the left fore is ending the stance phase, the right hind has started the stance phase and the right fore is starting the stance phase.

Trot

The trot is a **two beat gait**. While riding a trotting horse you can hear the hoof beats *one, two, one, two...* This is because in trot the four hooves land in diagonal pairs i.e. the front fore and diagonally opposite hind hoof land together, then the other front fore and diagonally opposite hind hoof land together.

There is a **period of suspension** (where no hooves are touching the ground) each time the horse 'jumps' from one diagonal pair to the other.

The footfalls of trot

The four hooves land two at a time in trot, one diagonally opposite pair, then a period of suspension, then the other diagonally opposite pair, then a period of suspension...

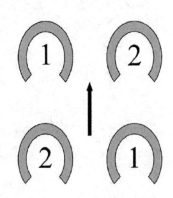

Riding the trot is more difficult than the walk (and some people believe more difficult than the canter) because a horse's back 'bumps' the rider almost directly upwards during each period of suspension, and as you know, what goes up must come down! Also a horse's back dips alternately on each side as the hind leg on each side swings forward under the body (during the swing phase for that particular leg). The rider has to learn how to 'absorb' all of the movement that is happening underneath them otherwise the trot can be very uncomfortable for both the rider and their horse. This is covered in detail in the section **Riding the trot**.

Like the walk, the trot is a *symmetrical* gait because the horse carries out the same actions with both sides of their body.

Picture right - you can see the horse's hip dipping on the right hand side as the right hind leg swings forward under the body.

Picture below - you can clearly see the period of suspension as the horse 'jumps' from one diagonal pair of legs to the other diagonal pair of legs. This is what propels you upwards in the trot.

Canter

The canter is a three beat gait. While riding a cantering horse you can hear the hoof beats one, two, three, one, two, three... This is because in canter two of the four hooves land separately and the other two land as a pair i.e. first a hind hoof lands, followed by the other hind hoof at the same time as the diagonally opposite fore, followed by the other fore.

Then there is a **_period of suspension_** (when all four legs are 'gathered' together under the horse's body) before a single hind hoof lands again and so on.

The footfalls of canter

The stride starts as one hind hoof lands, followed by the other hind and diagonally opposite fore hoof which land at the same time as each other, finally the last fore hoof lands (which is called the 'leading leg'). Then there is a period of suspension and the stride begins again as one hind hoof lands.

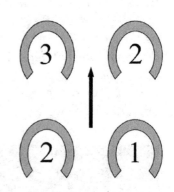

If a horse is cantering on a circle they should be 'leading' with the *inside* (the one closest to the inside of the circle) foreleg. Think about how you 'skipped' when you were young where you had one leg landing in front of the other. When a horse canters they 'roll over' the last foreleg down (the 'leading' leg) and they use this leg as a pivot point as they begin the period of suspension. If you watch a horse cantering free (without a rider) they will usually choose to lead with their inside leg on turns.

This horse is demonstrating the period of suspension in canter.

In order for a horse to achieve the correct lead on a right hand circle for example they would need to start the cycle with the *left* hind hoof touching down, followed by the *right* hind and *left* fore together, followed by the *right* fore (followed by the period of suspension). So the 'leading leg' is the *last* one to land in canter.

Again while canter is more difficult to ride than walk, many people prefer it to trotting. The canter does not have the same direct 'up' 'down' motion as the trot and therefore a rider does not 'rise to the canter'.

Instead the rider has to learn to absorb the more rounded dips and rises as the back of their horse goes through a more circular ('loop the loop') motion. This is further complicated because a horse is usually moving faster in canter (unless the horse is very well balanced) so unless a rider can move with their horse in canter they will feel very insecure indeed. If a horse is cantering on a circle the centrifugal force (the same thing that happens to your clothes in the washing machine on the spin cycle) further adds to this feeling of insecurity. How to overcome this problem and others is covered in detail in the section ***Riding the canter***.

Canter is an *asymmetrical* gait because the two sides of the horse do different things to each other (depending on which leg is 'leading').

This horse is cantering to the left. Her left hind and right fore are a pair. Her left fore is the leading leg and is about to land. Her weight will 'roll over' that leading leg and then the period of suspension will begin.

Both of these horses are also cantering to the left. They are slightly earlier in the stride than the horse in the previous picture. Their left hind's and right fore's are just about to touch down together.

Riding the walk

The walk is generally thought to be the easiest gait to ride because it is the slowest gait and there is *no period of suspension*. But you still need to make sure that you are riding it well and most riders can vastly improve how they ride the walk. As always it is important to start with the foundations.

Problems with the walk occur when a horse has not been taught to maintain speed in 'self-carriage' (see the **Horse Rider's Mechanic website article *What is 'self-carriage'?***). In this case 'self-carriage' means that the horse should maintain the same speed without having to be continuously slowed down by the reins or pushed on by the rider's legs.

When a horse is not walking in 'self-carriage' the rider might get into the habit of continuously fiddling with, or pulling on, the reins (if their horse is 'too forward going') or shove with their seat and continuously 'push their horse on' with their legs (if their horse is 'not forward going enough').

Teaching a horse how to move in the various gaits in 'self-carriage' is very important both for your riding enjoyment and your horse's welfare.

Improving how a rider rides the walk *initially involves learning to do less* for many riders. A rider needs to allow their pelvis to be moved *by their horse* so that in turn their horse can move their own back freely. This is simple to do once you know how.

What should happen...

- Your pelvis should move with the movement of your horse's back, in fact your horse's back should move your pelvis not vice versa.
- You should be able to feel your horse's back alternately dip on one side and then the other, this should be felt through your seat bones which are situated at the bottom end of your pelvis.

Your seat bones are located at the bottom of your pelvis. You must allow the movement of your horse's back to move them, rather than try to move your horse with your seat.

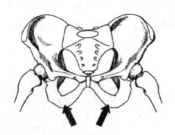

What should not happen...

- Pushing and shoving with your seat, this usually occurs if a horse is deemed 'not forward going enough'. Typically a rider tends to 'nag' with their seat and also their legs in this case.
- Bracing your pelvis against the movement of your horse, this usually occurs if a horse is 'too forward going'. Typically a rider tends to brace their seat and hang on to the reins in this case.

Walk lesson 1: Moving your seat with your horse in walk

This is a description of what you are aiming to feel, starting with the horse's *left* hind leg swinging forward:

- As the horse's *left* hind leg swings forward through the air (as part of the swing phase) the horse's back dips on that side.
- This is because as the *left* hind leg swings forward the belly swings from *left* to *right* (picture a).
- It may help you to remember this if you think of the hind leg 'kicking' the belly out of the way as it swings forward.
- As the *left* hind leg touches down and the horse's body moves forward over that leg (as part of the stance phase) the horse's back lifts on the left side as the belly swings back to the *left* (picture b).

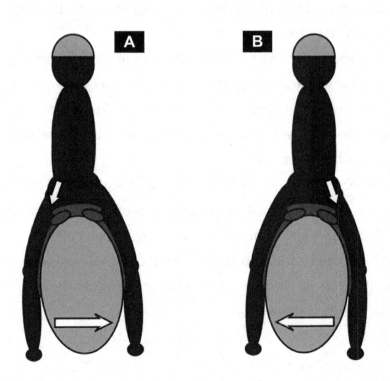

- If your seat bones truly follow this movement you will feel each seat bone dip as your horse's hind leg swings forward under the body, the belly swings away and your horse's back lowers. Then you will feel it lift as the horse's hind leg touches down, the belly swings back and your horse's back lifts.
- It may help to think of your seat bones 'peddling backwards'.

If you have never felt this and you suspect that you have been moving incorrectly up to now it is time to do something about it.

Learning to move your seat with your horse in walk:

- As your horse is walking on a long rein completely relax your pelvis. If you have been pushing and shoving with your seat in the past your legs will probably have been joining in as well so try to stop them from moving and let them simply 'hang'.
- For now you are aiming to do the complete opposite of what you have been doing, you are aiming to stop any forced movement and you are aiming to 'listen' with your body to what your horse's body is doing. You can only do this if you stop trying to move your pelvis and legs and *let your horse move you.*
- If your horse stops moving forward as you become stiller it is because your horse is not trained to go forward properly in self-carriage and maintain that speed without constant 'nagging' reminders.
- If you are used to 'dictating' with your body you will at first find it difficult to 'let go'. Work on it because the rewards are immense, not just for you but for your horse.

- Once you have learned the correct feeling you can experiment with re-engaging some of the muscles in this area but for now you are aiming to do nothing while you learn to feel what your horse's back is doing.

For many riders this is the first time they have released their pelvis while riding and it can be a revelation for them and their horse. Sensitive horses in particular start to relax more as they feel their rider start to move with them rather than against them.

As already mentioned, riders of horses that are deemed 'too forward going' tend to 'ride with the brakes on' by stiffening their pelvis. This simply makes their already tense horse even more so. These riders need to do the same as the above scenario, relax and let the horse's back move their pelvis. A horse that is tense also needs to be taught to walk in self-carriage but this time they need to learn to wait for the 'go faster' aid.

Learning to feel, through your pelvis, what your horse's back is doing can be a revelation for both you and your horse.

A great way to consolidate this lesson (but you will need an assistant) is to do the following:

- Call out left (or right) to your assistant each time you feel the left (or right) hind leg move under your horse and you feel your seat bone on the same side dip. Your assistant should see the correct hind leg swinging forward as you call 'left' (or 'right') and confirm that what you are feeling is correct.

Quick summary of this lesson: In walk, let any tension in your pelvis and your legs go. Feel your horse's back move your seat, you are aiming to feel each seat bone dip as your horse's hind leg on the same side swings forward through the air.

You are ready to move on to the next lesson when you can truly feel the movement of your horse's back through your seat bones/pelvis and if possible (because this depends on if you have assistant) correctly identify when each back leg of your horse swings forward under the body by feel alone.

An assistant can help by confirming what you feel. You can describe what you are experiencing and they can describe what they see. This process teaches you to be more aware of what you are feeling.

Walk lesson 2: The balance position in halt and walk

For this lesson you will need a neck strap fitted to your horse to aid your balance and prevent you either giving your horse a pull in the mouth or prevent you landing heavily on your horse's back. This neck strap will be needed for several of the following lessons so take a little time now to get it right.

Plaited hay bale twine or 'washing line' rope is usually fine and most horses accept it without a problem. An exception can be horses that have been ridden using a neck strap in place of reins in which case they will tend to stop every time you apply pressure to the strap, in this situation you may have to manage by holding the mane.

The neck strap needs to be thin and long enough for you to hold at the same time as your reins. It is best if it is adjustable so that you can shorten and lengthen it.

For my lessons and riding clinics I have several lengths of 'washing line' cord (usually sold in DIY/hardware stores), each cut to about 1.5m long (about 5 feet) with the ends taped off with electrical insulation tape (to stop fraying). This is tied around the neck of the horse using a 'reef knot'. If you prefer, a 'horseman's string' sold by various natural horsemanship trainers also works very well. An old rein, with extra holes punched into it (as long as the buckle is good and strong) is another option.

A reef knot

If your horse is sensitive you can put a sheepskin sleeve on part of the cord/strap so that this, rather than the thin cord or strap, contacts the base of your horse's neck when you are holding it.

If you are an instructor and you plan to incorporate this training tool into your teaching and you have lesson horses, I suggest you set up something more permanent and comfortable for your horse/s. A breastplate (this item of gear has different names in different countries i.e. a stockman's breastplate, hunting breastplate etc.) works well in this case. You can then fasten some cord (or a 'grab strap') to this.

A breastplate can be a more permanent solution. You can then fasten some cord (or a 'grab strap') to this.

Note: A 'grab strap' fastened in the usual place (i.e. the 'D' rings at the front of most 'English' style saddles) **is not** suitable. In this case, because it is fastened to the saddle it is positioned too close to the rider. A 'grab strap' fastened in this way can also be dangerous because saddle  'D's' are not usually designed to take much pulling pressure, they are actually designed to fasten saddle bags or a breastplate to, nothing more.

The balance position is crucial to improving you as a rider. Whatever your style of riding, you may have ridden in this position before. For example if you have ridden cross country jumps or even 'show jumped' in the past you will probably be familiar with it. Endurance riders also often ride in this position (while trotting or cantering) in order to change pressure points on themselves and their horse throughout a long ride.

Many riders though have never ridden in this balance position before so it is not surprising that some riders have issues with their balance. Once you have learned how to do this through the various gaits you will be amazed at the improvement in your riding. In this lesson we are going to start right at the beginning by learning how to balance at a standstill and then in walk.

You are now going to stand in the stirrups and stay standing up, balanced.

Learning the balance position in halt and walk:

- Ask your horse to stand still.
- Raise yourself up in the stirrups.
- Make sure your ankles, knees and hips are flexed, not stiff and straight (you may find it helpful to think about the position of someone when skiing downhill and imagine yourself in that position - see also the picture in the section *Standing trot lesson 1: Standing and staying balanced in trot*).
- Your legs should not be gripping at all, they should simply drape around your horse.

- Notice how your lower legs have to be directly underneath you in order to maintain this standing balanced position, as soon as your legs move too far forward or too far back you will lose balance.

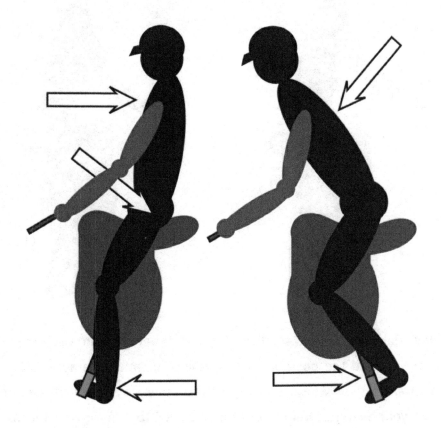

- From this position stand up onto the balls of your feet, raise your heels and notice how insecure you feel (picture a, next picture).
- Now drop your heels as far as they will go (picture b, next picture) and notice how your seat starts to drop back into the saddle and you start to lose balance (stop yourself from flopping down onto your horse's back). If you have very stiff ankles you may not be able to drop your heels far enough to experiment with this feeling. Don't worry if you cannot, it isn't essential.

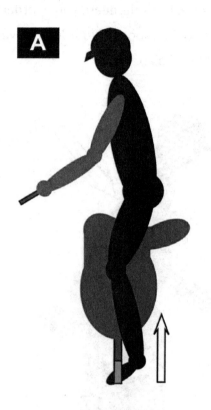

- Now make smaller and smaller adjustments between the two extremes until you find the position that is best. You should be able to find a neutral position where you can comfortably stay standing balanced, with your heels just below your toes, about 1 to 2 cm or ½ to 1 inch.

- Your hips, knees and ankles should be slightly flexed and able to absorb any movement. These three joints act as shock absorbers when riding.

- At this stage, if you cannot clear the saddle while at the same time allowing your heels to drop slightly then your stirrups are *too long*. Believe it or not, by initially shortening the stirrup length you will reap dividends later on! (see the **Horse Rider's Mechanic website article** *Your stirrup length*).

This rider's stirrups are slightly too long which means that there is not enough bend in her knee.

- There should be equal weight going down into each foot, with both sides of your feet loaded equally across the stirrup. This point is particularly important because many riders inadvertently roll their foot and ankle to the outside. If pain is experienced in the outside of your ankle when riding then this could be what is happening (see ***Horse Rider's Mechanic Workbook 1: Your Position*** for a detailed explanation of this).
- Next, while your horse is still immobile, you are going to practice lowering your seat back into the saddle. ***This step is very important.***
- From this standing position, rather than thinking about *'sitting down'* think about *'kneeling down'* and *lower* your seat back into the saddle.
- If you think *'kneel down'* as you return your seat to the saddle you will be able to maintain the *engagement* in your lower leg whereas if you think *sit down* your lower legs may swing forward from the knees or even the hips (especially if you tend to be stiff in your joints) and your lower leg will become 'disengaged'. This notion of *'kneeling down'* rather than *sitting down* is something you will need to utilise later in the trot lessons so practice this until you have it perfected.

If you think 'kneel down' as you return your seat to the saddle you will be able to maintain the engagement in your lower leg.

- Once you have mastered the balance position at standstill you can try it at walk, still holding the neck strap. You should feel the muscles in the front of your thighs working and the tendons that run from your calves to your heels (the Achilles tendons), stretching. Allow this stretch to happen but don't overdo it, have frequent breaks, or you will get too sore. If you have 'wobbly' joints make sure you do not allow your heels to drop *too* far, work on keeping them only about 1 to 2 cm (½ to 1 inch) below the balls of your feet.

If you have overly stiff joints or overly loose joints see Horse Rider's Mechanic Workbook 1: Your Position for more information about how this will affect your riding.

- Work up to letting go of the neck strap while remaining standing balanced in the walk.
- Check that you are absorbing the movement of your horse into your hips, knees and ankle joints correctly, slightly flexed rather than stiff and straight. A common scenario is a tendency to brace and/or grip with the knees. Mentally check that you are not doing this by turning your attention to your knees and thinking about the feeling in them.

Quick summary of this lesson: Starting at a standstill, stand in the stirrups and balance (holding on to a neck strap). Practice lowering yourself back into the saddle by 'kneeling' rather than 'sitting' down. Work up to balancing in walk, eventually without holding the neck strap.

You are ready to move on to the next lesson when you can stand balanced with ease without holding the neck strap while your horse walks forward.

Remember: if there is anything you do not understand or need help with after reading this book (or the others in this series) post a question on the Horse Rider's Mechanic Facebook page:

www.facebook.com/horseridersmechanic

Riding the trot

Remember the section *'The gaits'* described trotting as a two beat gait that has a *period of suspension* between the two beats and that the horse's back 'bumps' the rider upwards and forwards as the horse 'jumps' from one pair of diagonal footfalls to the other. This can make riding the trot quite difficult to do and most riders have room for improvement in terms of how they actually ride the trot. The following three sections should give you plenty of food for thought.

In trot your horse's back moves you up and <u>forwards</u> and down and <u>forwards</u>. In rising trot you use the momentum provided by your horse to 'rise' to the trot.

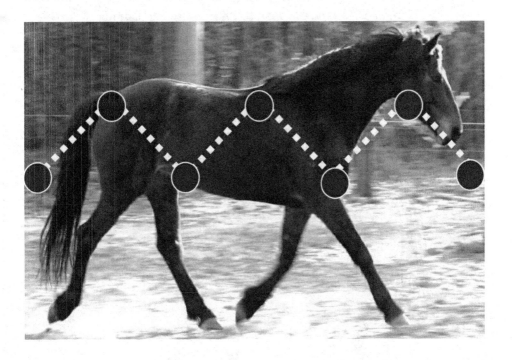

Individual horses vary enormously as to how comfortable they are in the trot. This is partly due to natural ability and breeding, (the conformation

31

of some horses allows better movement), partly due to training (a horse's way of moving improves in quality with the correct training) and partly due to the rider (a horse will usually stiffen/hollow their back, lift their head and shorten their stride in response to an unbalanced rider).

There are three ways of riding the trot, the most common being rising (often called posting in the US) and sitting. The third, standing trot, which in jumping or eventing circles it is also known as the 'two point seat' (because the rider's weight is transferred to their legs, as opposed to the 'three point seat', the term used to describe the usual sitting position), is an invaluable exercise that riders can use to improve the other trots (rising and sitting) and indeed their riding in general.

A horse will usually stiffen/hollow their back, lift their head and shorten their stride in response to an unbalanced rider.

Research carried out at the University of Veterinary Medicine Vienna's Movement Science Group showed that the two point seat (standing trot) is the least stressful for the horse and provides the most stability for the rider. The sitting trot is at the opposite end of the scale, with rising trot in between. So learning to stand to the trot is very worthwhile indeed whatever riding discipline you follow.

I have been using the standing trot as a means of improving a rider's balance for many years, to great effect. This section, **Riding the trot,** should contain many 'light bulb moments' for you and your horse.

In my lessons and clinics I address the rising trot first, followed by the standing trot and then the sitting trot. I address them in this order because the rising trot usually needs some 'tweaking' and a good rising trot is important in order to learn the standing trot effectively. In turn, once standing trot has been fully mastered it can be used to improve the sitting trot (or indeed to teach a rider sitting trot from scratch).

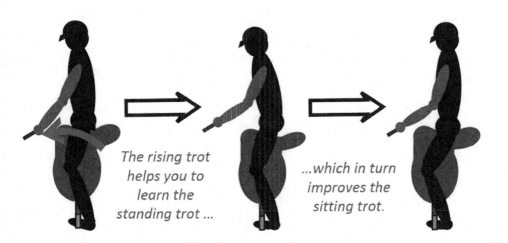

The rising trot helps you to learn the standing trot ...

...which in turn improves the sitting trot.

Rising trot

Many riders know and regularly use *rising* trot. Ridden correctly it is a way of using the upward 'bump' that their horse provides as the back leg (of their horse) comes underneath the body, coupled with the downward force of gravity, to move in time with their horse.

Another way of putting it is that instead of simply bouncing up and down on a horse's back (very uncomfortable, painful even, for both the rider and horse) the rider times their movements so that they are perfectly in synchronisation with the up/forward and down/backward movement of their horse's back.

When people are first taught to ride they may have learned how to rise to the trot via an uncomfortable combination of trial and error coupled with someone telling them to 'rise up' and 'sit down' in time with their horse. For many riders this is as much information about rising to the trot that they ever receive, therefore most riders go on to a lifetime of riding without ever understanding the finer details of rising to the trot.

What should happen...

- Your seat should rise up and forward and down and back (rather than straight up in the air and down again). It should follow an arch shape with the top end of your thigh swinging forwards and backwards.
- Your seat should land softly in the saddle and rise up and forward again with very little effort.
- Your hands should stay still which means that your elbows should open and close slightly as your seat goes up and forward and down and back.
- All of this should happen in *precise* time with the movements of your horse's back. This involves muscular effort when carried out properly

however, once you learn how to move efficiently and how to harness the upward movement of your horse and the downward force of gravity to your advantage, it becomes much easier. In time, as your muscles and skills develop, it becomes almost effortless.

Your hands should stay still which means that in rising trot your elbows should open and close as your seat goes up and down.

What should not happen...

- Becoming overly tired (other than what can be explained by lack of fitness).
- Upsetting your horse.
- 'Double bumping' where your seat lands a fraction of a second too early, before the upwards bump from your horse happens.
- Losing the stirrups (especially the inside one on a circle).
- Heavy landing.
- Rising too high.
- Rising too low.
- Getting 'left behind', in which case you will tend to land too far back in the saddle.
- Twisting your upper body as you rise.

This rider is rising too high and is getting left behind the movement. Because of this she is using the reins to balance herself which in turn means that her horse is unbalanced.

Rising trot lesson 1: Rising to the trot with accuracy and strength

As a rider rises to the trot their knee joint should open and close with their lower leg staying 'engaged' underneath them. The 'knee end' of their thigh should be still while the 'hip end' of their thigh should describe a small arch. Another way of describing this is that the thigh should behave like the upside down pendulum of an old fashioned clock, with the knee staying still and the hip swinging forward to describe part of a small circle.

The 'knee end' of your thigh should be still while the 'hip end' of your thigh should describe a small arch when you rise to the trot.

Therefore 'rising' to the trot is not a very accurate term for what you actually do, because if you literally go up and down you tend to get left behind the movement of your horse (because your horse is moving forward). If instead you work on getting your thigh to work correctly, rising becomes much easier and smoother as you move *forward* with your horse. So, each time your seat leaves the saddle your hips should move in a forwards arch.

Learning to rise to the trot with accuracy and strength:

- Ask your horse to trot and begin rising (if you are on a circle check you are on the correct diagonal but if you are not sure how to do this it is covered in *Rising trot lesson 4* so don't worry about it too much for now).
- As much as it is safe to do so turn your attention to thinking about 'engaging' the muscles at the lower end of your thighs to control your 'rise' and your 'sit'.

Engage the muscles at the lower end of your thighs to control your rise and your sit.

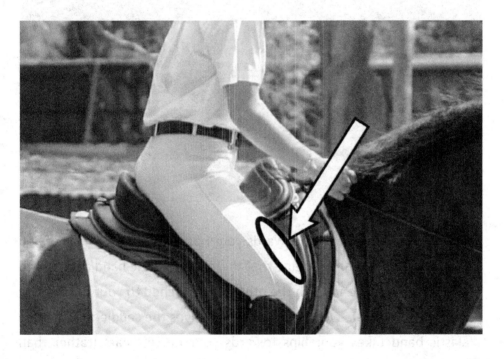

- Instead of simply allowing the upward 'bump' of your horse to throw you up and gravity to bring you back down again you are now controlling the speed and height of your rising and sitting by using the muscles in your thighs. If you have not already been doing this you may find it very tiring at first. The good news is that your thigh muscles are usually very quick to respond and quickly adapt to this increased workload.

As you rise take your hips towards your horse's ears. For those of you that like visualisations imagine that there is an elastic band attached to your navel at one end, with the other end attached to your horse's poll (between the ears).

- As you rise take your hips towards your horse's ears. For those of you that like visualisations imagine that there is an elastic band attached to your navel at one end, with the other end attached to your horse's poll (between his ears). Every time your seat leaves the saddle this invisible elastic band takes your hips towards your horse's ears (rather than straight up in the air). Remember, your horse is moving forward therefore you must too, or you will be left behind the movement.
- Your shoulders should be just slightly in front of your hips through both the rise and the sit phases.

- Your knees should never fully open. If they do you are rising too high and/or your stirrups are too long.
- You should find that you can now control how high you rise (you should now be able to rise higher and faster or slower and lower if you wish). This does not mean that you *should* be rising high and fast, you should in fact be rising only as far as is necessary. But you now have the means to control your rising.

Quick summary of this lesson: In rising trot turn your attention to engaging the muscles in your thighs to control the speed and height of your rising. Make sure your hips move towards your horse's ears as you rise.

You are ready to move on to the next lesson when you can rise to the trot with accuracy and strength, without tiring. Also when you can move forward with your horse without getting left behind the movement.

Rising trot lesson 2: Landing softly in rising trot

Now that you have more control over your rising you can further improve so that you land as *softly* as possible. You may also have noticed that sometimes (or always) a 'double bump' is felt when your seat returns to the saddle (picture a, next picture). 'Double bumping' occurs if you land a fraction of a moment too soon. The first bump is your seat landing in the saddle and the second is your horse's back bumping you up again as the hind leg comes underneath the body.

Instead your seat should touch the saddle at *exactly* the same time that your horse bumps you up again and no 'double bump' should be felt. Your thigh muscles control the speed and the height of the rising and lowering, enabling you to land softly and gently and at *exactly* the right moment.

If you are not folding at the knee correctly you will also tend to lose balance and fall backwards and land too heavily so the previous lesson and this one should sort out any such problems.

Learning to land softly in rising trot:

- Ask your horse to trot, begin rising and turn as much of your attention as it is safe to do so to how you 'rise' and 'sit'.
- Remember how in *Walk lesson 2: The balance position in halt and walk* you learned to 'kneel down' rather that 'sit down' as you returned your seat to the saddle.
- Doing this means that you lower yourself by 'folding' your joints (picture b, next picture), especially your knees, which allows your seat to *lower* into the saddle rather than 'fall' backwards and land towards the back of the saddle.

- Now, with your thigh muscles engaged think 'kneel' each time you are about to return to the saddle. This will help you to land in the correct part of the saddle, the middle, rather than towards the back. Also any 'double bumping' should be eliminated and your horse will find you much easier to carry.

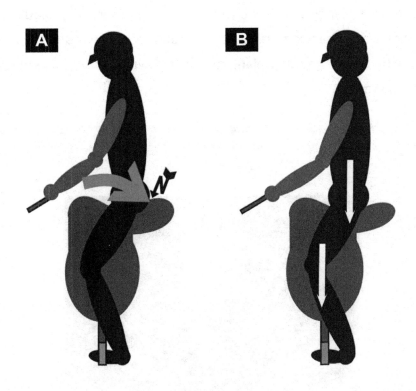

Quick summary of this lesson: In rising trot turn your attention to how you land in the saddle. Think 'kneel' rather than 'sit'. Aim to land in the middle of your saddle (rather than towards the back) at exactly the same movement that your horse 'bumps' you back up again.

You are ready to move on to the next lesson when you can land softly with your seat touching down in the middle of your saddle rather than towards the back.

Rising trot lesson 3: Lowering your centre of gravity in rising trot

In rising trot your centre of gravity should stay as low as possible. This is because when your centre of gravity is high you are at risk of losing balance (see the **Horse Rider's Mechanic website article** *Your centre of gravity*). In rising trot, the moment your seat leaves the saddle your centre of gravity begins to rise, but you can reduce any potential loss of balance by allowing your weight to travel down your legs as your seat leaves the saddle.

In this picture the rider is rising too high (her knee is almost straight) but she is also allowing her heels to rise as she rises. This means that her centre of gravity is too high.

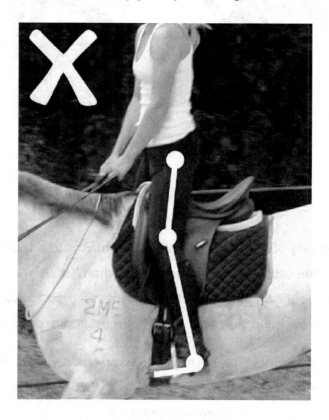

If you watch people riding and you concentrate on what their heels are doing as they rise to the trot you will often see that their heel actually *rises* slightly as their seat leaves the saddle. This is actually incorrect as their heel should *drop* slightly as the weight that was on their seat bones transfers down through their legs. If the knees are not gripping, this weight should travel all the way down their legs and into their heels, which will dip to absorb this downward change of weight. Riders that allow their heels to travel upwards as they rise are *pushing up* with their feet instead. Often riders do this simply because no one has ever explained to them that the opposite should in fact occur.

To exacerbate this problem, when a rider's stirrups are too long it is impossible for them to allow the heels to dip as they rise because in order for them to clear the saddle (as they rise) they have to stand up on the balls of their feet. This puts the rider in a precarious position in terms of where their centre of gravity is.

Learning to lower your centre of gravity in rising trot:

- Ask your horse to trot, begin rising, check that you are rising with accuracy and strength and that you are landing softly (and 'cleanly') and then turn as much of your attention as it is safe to do so to your heels.
- Think about whether your heels are rising along with your seat (incorrect) or lowering slightly as your seat leaves the saddle (correct). If they are not lowering as you rise concentrate on letting them 'drop' as your seat leaves the saddle.
- If you have been riding for some time with your heels moving in the wrong direction as you rise, trying to do the opposite can be rather like

trying to pat the top of your head while you rub your belly. Persevere and it will eventually feel 'normal'.

In these two pictures you can see that the rider is allowing her heels to rise slightly as she rises up and forward (picture a) (incorrect), and allowing her heels to drop slightly (picture b) (correct).

Quick summary of this lesson: In rising trot turn your attention to your heels. They should go down (not up) as your seat leaves the saddle.

You are ready to move on to the next lesson when you can feel your heels lower slightly as your seat rises up and forwards in rising trot.

Rising trot lesson 4: Two ways to change the diagonal

Make sure you read the **Horse Rider's Mechanic website article** *Rising diagonals*. Even if you do not generally ride in circles you need to work the muscles on both sides of your horse's body equally. You do this by changing your rising diagonal in rising trot.

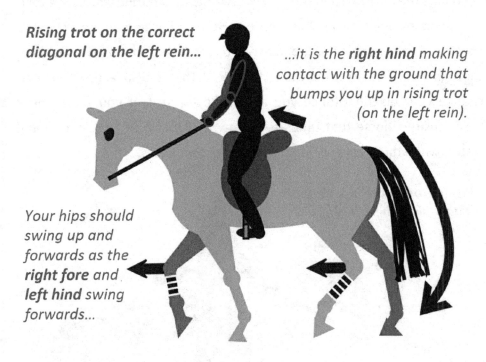

Rising trot on the correct diagonal on the left rein...

*...it is the **right hind** making contact with the ground that bumps you up in rising trot (on the left rein).*

*Your hips should swing up and forwards as the **right fore** and **left hind** swing forwards...*

When you are riding in a circle (in rising trot) it is generally thought correct to rise out of the saddle as your horse's *outside* shoulder (and *inside* hind leg) swing forward. So, if you are on the *left* rein (that is, you and your horse are travelling anticlockwise and the left rein of the bridle is on the *inside* of the circle), your seat will swing up and forward as your horse's *right fore* and *left hind* leg swing forward. Your seat will be in the saddle as your horse's *right fore* and *left hind* leg (the same legs) are in contact with the ground.

If you are rising on the wrong diagonal the usual way to change it is to sit for two beats instead of one. You would ride the following: up, down, up, *down, down*, up, and this then causes you to rise as the opposite pair of diagonal legs moves forward. Sitting for two beats is the accepted way to change the diagonal and the way you should do it during a dressage test.

A good exercise to further improve your rising and to improve the control of your position and balance is to practice changing the diagonal through two 'rises' rather than two 'sits'. This is also a good way to change your diagonal (once you are proficient at it) if you are riding a very sensitive horse that tends to hollow their back, or anticipate going faster, when they feel the rider sit down for two beats.

Rising trot on the incorrect diagonal on the left rein...

*The rider's hips are swinging up and forwards as the **left fore** and **right hind** swing forwards...*

Learning another way to change the diagonal in rising trot:

- Start by asking your horse to trot and begin rising. Turn as much of your attention as it is safe to do so to your rising and sitting.
- Say out loud, or in your head, 'up, down, up, down', in time with your rising and sitting. Then say 'up, down, *up, up*, down', while you match with your seat what you are saying/thinking.
- Notice how you need to use your core (abdominal) muscles to do this.
- You might get left behind slightly on the second beat, so it is a good idea to use a neck strap at first.

*Down,
up,
up,
down.*

- With practice it becomes easier and you will add another useful skill to your riding repertoire.
- In the final section about trotting you will learn how to always rise on the correct diagonal by feel alone, but first you need to work through the following sections about standing trot and sitting trot.

Quick summary of this lesson: In rising trot change the rising diagonal through two 'rises' rather than two 'sits'.

You are ready to move on to the next lesson when you can change your diagonal by staying up for an extra beat (rather than sitting for an extra beat) without getting left behind the movement of your horse.

Standing trot

You may not have heard of 'standing' trot before or you may know it as 'the two point seat'. Standing trot is where the rider stands balanced in their stirrups. Instead of rising up and down, the rider 'absorbs' the up and down movement of their horse into their ankles, knees and hips. Another way of thinking of this style of riding the trot is that the seat 'hovers' over the saddle.

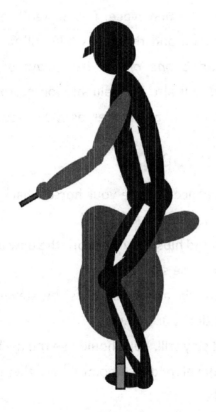

Riders who regularly use this style of riding the trot are generally jump riders, event riders and endurance riders and they benefit greatly from developing this skill. These riders use this position for canter as well as trot and this is one of the lessons in the section about canter. In the case of jump and event riders they employ a more forward position than you are about to do in the following lessons, but the benefits are the same.

Most other riders are never taught this balance dependant style of riding the walk, trot and canter and therefore they miss out on the invaluable lessons it brings.

Riding in this position relies on using the core muscles of the abdomen, the muscles in the legs (particularly the thighs) and on having the balance to stay 'up'. This position, as well as needing the rider to employ muscular effort and balance in the first place, further (and rapidly) *develops* the muscles of the abdomen and the legs while still *further improving* the balance. *This position is one of the best ways of speeding up your development as a rider.* It also is invaluable for improving the rising trot, sitting trot (believe it or not) and canter, as you will soon see.

What should happen...

- You should stay balanced above your horse's back with your seat not actually touching the saddle.
- Your ankles, knees and hips should absorb the upwards and downwards movement of your horse's back.
- Your lower legs should act as 'anchors' by staying 'engaged' in the correct position under your body.
- Your hands should stay still. You should use the neck strap initially until your balance has developed to a point where there is no risk of falling back into the saddle.
- This exercise requires flexibility of the three pairs of shock absorbing joints *as well* as muscular effort from your legs and your abdominal core muscles. This can be quite difficult to achieve at first (even some experienced riders have trouble with it initially) but you will quickly improve and begin to reap the benefits.

You should use the neck strap initially until your balance has developed to a point where there is no risk of falling back into the saddle.

What should not happen...

- Becoming overly tired (other than what can be explained by a lack of fitness).
- Upsetting your horse.
- Pain (usually felt in the lower back area or the outside of the ankles).
- Losing balance (legs slip forwards or backwards, upper body tips forwards or backwards).

In this picture the rider has let her lower legs move too far forward and she has started to fall back into the saddle.

Standing trot lesson 1: Standing and staying balanced in trot

This requires quite a lot of suppleness and strength so it is important that you gradually increase the time spent doing this (rather than overdo it and make yourself sore). Even experienced and fit riders usually find this difficult at first, however it quickly becomes easier. You will need to use a neck strap (already described in **Walk lesson 2: The balance position in halt and walk**).

Learning to stand and stay balanced in trot:

- If possible start in an enclosed area such as a round yard or fenced arena.
- Initially take your stirrups up a couple of holes unless you already ride with shorter than average stirrups.

This is the minimum amount of 'bend' you will need in your hips, knees and ankles in order to stand balanced in your stirrups.

- Repeat *Walk lesson 2: The balance position in halt and walk* until you feel you are confident at standing balanced in the walk.
- Ask your horse to trot and start by rising to the trot.
- While you are rising, reach for and hold the neck strap and simultaneously stand up in your stirrups.
- The same principles apply when standing in the trot as for standing in the walk. However it is now more difficult because of the extra speed and the period of suspension in the trot (when your horse 'jumps' from one diagonal pair of legs to the other). This will cause your calves and Achilles tendons to stretch.
- Remember, your hips, knees and ankles should be flexed and should absorb the movement. Thinking of the position of a downhill skier might help.

- If you have been riding with your ankles rolled to the outside and you have not yet truly corrected them, now is when you will really feel this happening and you will probably feel a sharp pain in the *outside* of your ankle (see the section *Your ankles* in *Horse Rider's Mechanic Workbook 1: Your Position* for a detailed explanation about how your ankles should behave when riding).

- Gradually increase the length of time you stay standing. Switch back to rising to the trot frequently and before you feel any real pain.

- If you have floppy (loose) ankles you will need to consciously stop your ankles from flexing too much and allowing your heels to drop too far. You may need to temporarily or permanently 'strap' your ankles as described in *Your ankles* in *Horse Rider's Mechanic Workbook 1: Your Position*.

You may need to temporarily or even permanently strap your ankles.

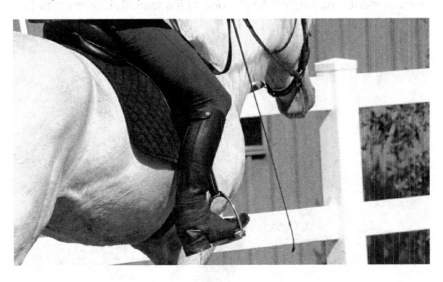

- If you have stiff ankles you will benefit even more from this exercise because your ankles will 'learn' how to flex a little more.

- Your legs should not be gripping at all and should simply drape around your horse. Your legs do have to come directly under your body in order to stand up and stay up. If your legs move forward, even just a little you will lose balance and you will start to fall back into the saddle (that is why you need a neck strap initially).

- Once you are able to balance standing in trot without needing the neck strap it is still a good idea to keep it in place for a while and hold on to it lightly. You will also need it for some of the upcoming lessons.

Quick summary of this lesson: From rising trot (with a neck strap fitted to your horse) stand in the stirrups and balance. Gradually build up the length of time you stay up in your stirrups.

You are ready to move on to the next lesson when you can stand balanced in the stirrups without holding the neck strap while your horse trots.

Standing trot lesson 2: Maintaining this position through changes of speed and direction

The initial phase of learning to stand and stay balanced in trot is the most difficult. Now that you have this skill you can further improve by practicing this position as your horse changes speed and direction (in the trot).

Learning to maintain this position through changes of speed and direction:

- Using the neck strap, ask your horse to trot faster for a few strides (using a 'go forward' leg aid) and then to slow down (using a 'slow down' rein aid).
- At first you may find it difficult from this standing balanced position but it will get easier. When you have mastered the above you can ask your horse to change direction, for example, if you are riding in an arena you could start with a large figure of eight, working up to a smaller figure of eight.

Quick summary of this lesson: While standing and balancing in the stirrups at trot practice changes of speed and then changes of direction.

You are ready to move on to the next lesson when you can stand balanced in the stirrups, without holding the neck strap, while your horse speeds up and slows down (in trot) and changes direction.

Standing trot lesson 3: Feeling for the movement of your horse's back

Remember how in *Walk lesson 1: Moving your seat with your horse in walk* you learned how to feel your horse's hind leg swing underneath the body by feeling your seat bone on the same side dip. In trot your horse's back also dips as each hind leg swings forward under the body. Trotting in a standing balanced position is the best way to learn how to feel this happening so that you can then use this skill (for both you and your horse's benefit) in the other two styles of riding the trot.

In trot your horse's back also dips as each hind leg swings forward under the body.

Learning to feel for the movement of your horse's back:

- In standing trot turn as much of your attention as it is safe to do so to your ankles and heels.
- Remember, in trot, the belly of your horse swings to the other side as each back leg swings forward through the air.

- When standing balanced in trot you should be able to feel the alternating dipping of each side of your horse's back.
- If you are allowing your weight to travel down your legs without blocking the movement by gripping or bracing your knees you will feel each heel dip slightly in time with this dipping of your horse's back.

In standing trot you should be able to feel each of your heels in turn dip slightly more than the other one as your horse's belly swings away and their hip drops on that side.

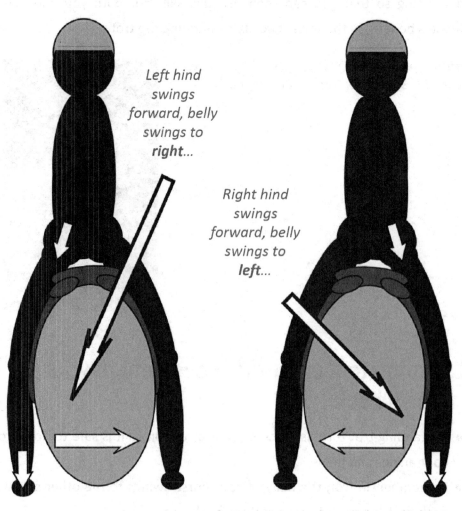

*Left hind swings forward, belly swings to **right**...*

*Right hind swings forward, belly swings to **left**...*

- Therefore you can now tell where each leg is during each stride by feel alone!
- If you have an assistant, call out 'left' as you feel your horse's left hind leg swing forward under the body (and you feel your heel on that same side dip a bit more than the other one). They should see the left hind leg of your horse swing forward as you call 'left'.
- If you have a problem feeling this try deliberately 'stepping' from your left foot to your right foot as your horse trots. You can only be wrong 50% of the time with this one so if it feels wrong switch from stepping 'left, right, left, right' to stepping 'right, left, right, left'. You will find that you learn to feel when you are moving in time with your horse rather than against the movement of your horse. Once you have it you will be able to feel it again and again.

Quick summary of this lesson: While standing and balancing in the stirrups at trot, turn as much of your attention as it is safe to do so to your ankles and heels. Feel one and then the other dip as your horse's hind leg on the same side swings forward under the body.

You are ready to move on to the next lesson when you can feel and identify when each of your horse's hind legs swing forward under the body by feeling your ankle and heel on the same side dip.

You are now ready to learn how to sit to the trot or to improve your sitting trot.

Sitting trot

In sitting trot the rider keeps their seat in the saddle throughout the 'up' and the 'down' phase of their horse's stride. This involves the correct weighting of their seat and legs, much effort of their abdominal muscles in particular *and* flexibility in the pelvis in two different directions at once (no wonder it is difficult!).

Many riders regard a comfortable sitting trot as an unattainable goal! Sitting trot would have to be the biggest 'bug bear' of riders. Many riders avoid it altogether by only ever rising to the trot (some riders even avoid *trotting* altogether by teaching their horse to go straight from walk to canter and vice versa!). Dressage and event riders of course cannot avoid trotting and when they reach a certain level where *sitting* trot is required

they sometimes reach a 'roadblock'. This is exacerbated because dressage horses in particular are bred to have big springy extravagant movement that is particularly difficult to sit to (ironically).

Beginners are not usually taught to do sitting trot unless they are riding a super smooth moving horse but when they reach the stage where their instructor feels they are ready, the information they tend to receive may be along the lines of 'sit down', 'sit still', 'don't bounce', 'relax'! etc. None of this is very useful information about how to *actually* ride this sometimes difficult movement. And if you think you have already mastered the sitting trot, wait until you ride a big moving dressage bred Warmblood before you tick this skill off as fully accomplished, because riding a smooth moving quarter horse for example just does not compare. In fact some quarter horses have been bred to be *so* smooth that rising is actually *more difficult* than sitting because a very smooth moving horse gives virtually no 'upwards bump' to push you up out of the saddle.

Conversely, if you are having problems with the sitting trot due to your horse having extravagant (or in some cases, harsh) movement it can be a good idea to try out the following lessons (**sitting trot lessons 1, 2** and **3**) on a horse with smoother movement (although not super smooth or you will not really learn anything). Then once you have mastered the required skills you can move back to your bigger moving horse and apply your new found knowledge and skills.

Most of the previous lessons are prerequisites for the following lessons for sitting trot. You will now be building on what you have learned so far.

What should happen...

- You should move *with* your horse (without bouncing), absorbing the movement of your horse's back into your lower and upper body, each area behaving differently.

- Your lower body should lengthen in one direction (downwards) while your upper body lengthens in the other direction (upwards).
- Your weight should be distributed between your seat and your feet. The weight of your legs should travel down from your pelvis to your feet.

Your lower body should lengthen in one direction (downwards) while your upper body lengthens in the other direction (upwards).

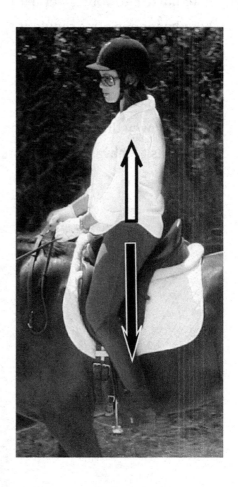

- There should be enough weight in your feet to keep your stirrups in place but you should *not be pressing down* into your stirrups because this pushes you *upwards* and leads to bouncing as your centre of gravity rises (see the **Horse Rider's Mechanic website article *Your centre of gravity***). There is *a whole world of difference* between allowing your weight to travel down your legs (correct) and pressing down through your legs (incorrect).

- Your upper body should be mainly upright and should give the appearance of being still while absorbing some of the movement from your horse into your lower back.

- Your hands and arms should stay still and soft.

- Your pelvis should *simultaneously* flex backwards and forwards while each seat bone (the 'rocker' at the bottom of each side of your pelvis) lifts and dips in time with the movement of your horse's back. This is primarily *why* the sitting trot can be so difficult to master, because the pelvis has to move in such a complex manner.

Your upper body should be mainly upright and should give the appearance of being still while absorbing some of the movement from your horse into your lower back. A good sitting trot gives the impression of being effortless when in fact it involves a lot of complex coordination and core muscle strength. It takes time to develop, give yourself time and you will get there.

This is why the sitting trot can be difficult to master. Your pelvis has to swing backwards and forwards (a) while simultaneously lifting and lowering in the other direction (b and c).

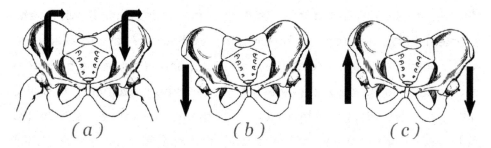

(a)   (b)   (c)

- You should feel each side of your horse's back dip alternately with your seat bones.
- The sitting trot requires the correct amount of flexibility of primarily your pelvis area coupled with flexibility of the other shock absorbing joints in your legs. At the same time you need strong abdominal muscles to achieve the correct 'movement' and to stay with your horse.

What should not happen...

- Becoming overly tired (other than what can be explained by a lack of fitness).
- Upsetting your horse.
- Bouncing.
- Losing the stirrups (especially the inside one on a circle).
- Pain (usually felt in the lower back area).
- Excessive leaning forwards or backwards.
- Pressing on the stirrups.

Sitting trot lesson 1: Weighting your seat bones and legs correctly

The name 'sitting' trot implies that the rider 'sits'. That is where the problem starts. Because the rider is thinking that they have to keep their seat in the saddle at all costs they tend to stiffen areas of the body that should instead be relaxed (enough to absorb the movement). It is also unhelpful that riders may be told to 'pull themselves into the saddle' (by holding on to the pommel of the saddle). This does nothing to teach them what they need to learn.

Commonly for most riders when trying to sit to the trot a vicious circle occurs. It starts with them starting to bounce. Then their legs start to creep up the sides of their horse in an effort to grip thinking this will keep them on.

When the lower leg begins to disengage the rider starts to feel insecure.

Commonly for most riders when trying to sit to the trot a vicious circle occurs. It starts with them starting to bounce. Then their legs start to creep up the sides of their horse in an effort to grip thinking this will keep them on.

Now their lower legs are 'disengaged' and their stirrups start to either clatter about on their feet or they lose them altogether, leading to more bouncing, gripping etc. Their centre of gravity is now too high and it is difficult to 'override' the unhelpful messages that are coming thick and fast from the brain. Messages such as 'hang on tighter', 'stiffen up' and other unhelpful suggestions! See the **Horse Rider's Mechanic website article *Your centre of gravity.***

Added to this their horse (quite understandably) may get upset and start to hollow and stiffen in the back which causes the rider to bounce even more. This may sound familiar to you and this can even happen to experienced riders although usually to a lesser degree.

There are lots of opinions about how a rider should sit to the trot but many of them are not very helpful. This section will show you a way that has worked for countless numbers of my clients over the years. Try it and if you follow the instructions it will work for you.

Learning to weight your seat bones and legs correctly:

- Start in standing trot. Ask your horse to trot as slowly as possible without falling back into a walk.
- 'Kneel down' from the standing position, *lowering* your seat into the saddle.
- Aim to keep a certain amount of weight going down into your feet as you 'sit' to the trot as this helps your legs to stay 'engaged'. This will require some extra muscular effort.
- Keeping your legs 'engaged' means that the movement of your horse is absorbed into your hips, knees and ankles and is directed down your legs rather than up and into your upper body.

'Kneel down' from the standing position, lowering your seat into the saddle.

70

- Experiment with just how much weight is needed in the balls of your feet to keep your legs 'engaged'. If your horse has a big springy movement you will need to have lots of flexibility in the joints of your legs (including your hips) and you will *almost* have to 'hover' over your horse's back. If your horse is smoother moving you will be able to 'release' more of your weight into your seat (but you will still need to keep your legs 'engaged').
- Once you have learned this technique you will find that you can then adapt to riding different horses with their different amounts of 'bounce'.
- If and when you feel yourself start to bounce, stand up again, which will re-distribute some weight back down your legs and will 're–engage' your legs.
- You may find that simply *starting* to stand up again, rather than actually standing all the way up, is enough to 're-engage' your legs.
- At this stage don't attempt to lengthen through your upper body or you will probably start to bounce. Just concentrate on learning how to arrange your lower body correctly for now.

If and when you feel yourself start to bounce, stand up again, which will re-distribute some weight back down your legs and will 're–engage' your legs.

- You may find that you can only get a few good strides and then you start to bounce again. Keep standing up, 'kneeling down', followed by standing again. With practice you will be able to go for longer periods of sitting down without bouncing.
- You are not aiming for perfection at this stage. If you try too hard you may become too stiff. You will need to complete the next lesson to further improve your sitting trot. For now you are just learning how to distribute your weight properly.
- If it helps, utilise your neck strap to help you stand up from a sitting trot (but not to 'pull' you down into the saddle, as this does not enable you to learn how to distribute your weight properly or move your pelvis correctly).

Quick summary of this lesson: From standing trot 'kneel down' but make sure your legs stay 'engaged' and underneath you. Keep standing back up again if and when you feel yourself start to bounce.

You are ready to move on to the next lesson when you can 'sit' to the trot for about ten or more strides without bouncing. Remember, you are not aiming for perfection at this stage.

Sitting trot lesson 2: Feeling the correct movement through your pelvis

Riders are often confused about how their pelvis should move when trying to sit to the trot. There is much discussion about whether a rider should allow their lower back to hollow or whether they should flatten their lower back.

Much of the information about riding assumes that people are all built the same and that they should all conform to an ideal position or way of doing things, riders with disabilities have proved that this is not the case. In particular, the lower back is an area that humans differ in quite remarkably, as some people are 'sway backed' and others are naturally straighter. Whatever your back conformation your pelvis needs to be able to move backwards and forwards in order to absorb the movement that is happening underneath you.

Humans differ enormously in body shape, in particular the lower back area. The diagram shows variations from the 'norm' in the human spine. Starting with normal on the left, then kyphosis (rounded upper back), too straight (not enough curvature), lordosis (very curved inwards) and then kyphosis and lordosis together. Other people have a certain amount of scoliosis (spine curvature to the side with lordosis and/or kyphosis).

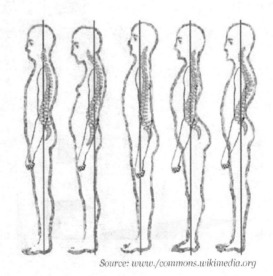

Source: www./commons.wikimedia.org

The other issue is that your horse's back dips and rises alternately on each side as each hind leg in turn swings under the body. This has already

73

been described several times throughout the course of this book. The rider's pelvis, *at the same time as having to flex backwards and forwards to absorb the upwards/downwards movement that is happening underneath them, has to dip and lift on each side alternately in time with the movements of their horse's back.* This is why the sitting trot is problematic for many people. The pelvis has to flex in both the vertical *and* horizontal plane at the same time! Don't worry, if you have worked through the lessons to this point you already have the tools to carry out this movement correctly.

When you can feel your pelvis moving in the forwards and backwards plane you can experiment with feeling your pelvis also moving in the other direction. You can tell this is happening when you can feel your heels alternately dip on each side as your horse's back dips.

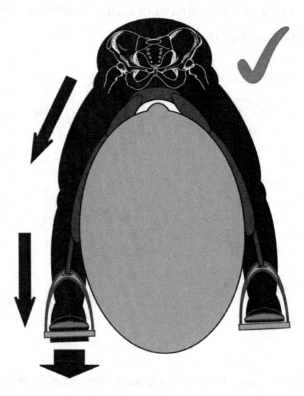

Learning to feel the correct movement through your pelvis:

- Firstly you are going to experiment with how flexible your lower back needs to be in order to absorb the upwards and downwards movement that is being generated by your horse.

- Now that you have improved the weighting of your seat and legs you should find that you are able to experiment without losing your balance or bouncing too much.

- For most riders at this stage it is about learning to relax the pelvis area more than they have done in the past. For now try relaxing this area totally if you can. This is just a starting point so that you can feel what happens when you let your horse move you. You should feel your pelvis moving more than it was before.

- Next, experiment with re-engaging your abdominal (core) muscles until they are firm but not stiff, loose but not floppy and your pelvis is still being moved by your horse.

For now try relaxing this area totally if you can. This is just a starting point so that you can feel what happens when you let your horse move you. You should feel your pelvis moving more than it was before.

- One of the criteria of becoming a good rider is learning to have the correct amount of muscle tension to achieve the middle ground between being too stiff and being too loose.
- Once you have worked out how to let your pelvis be moved in the backwards/forwards plane think about your heels and feel for the alternating dip as you did in standing trot.
- Once you can feel it this means that your pelvis is also moving correctly from side to side.

Once you have worked out how to let your pelvis be moved in the backwards/forwards plane think about your heels and feel for the alternating dip as you did in standing trot.

- Again, you may only be able to get the correct feeling for a few strides at a time. If you feel yourself starting to bounce, go back to standing in your stirrups for a few strides, or just prepare to stand as this may be enough to redistribute you weight (or go to rising trot).
- If you have an assistant call out 'left' as you feel your horse's left hind leg swing forward under their body (and you feel your seat bone and heel on the same side dip). Your assistant should see the left hind leg of your horse swing forward as you call 'left'.
- When you have achieved this and you can comfortably sit to the trot for a period of time without bouncing you have come a long way indeed!

Quick summary of this lesson: In sitting trot relax your abdominal muscles and let your horse flex your pelvis in the backwards / forwards plane. Then, when you have managed to do this and you have experimented with 're-engaging' your abdominal muscles so that you are not too wobbly (or too stiff), concentrate on feeling for the alternate dipping in your heels as you did in standing trot. When you have achieved both of the above this means that your pelvis is moving correctly.

You are ready to move on to the next lesson when, in sitting trot, you can feel and follow the alternating dip and lift of each side of your horses back while at the same time allowing your pelvis to flex backwards and forwards.

Sitting trot lesson 3: Sitting taller

Now to finish your improvement of the sitting trot. Sitting taller while sitting to the trot is 'the icing on the cake' for this movement. There is no point in trying to do this until your lower body is working correctly. This is because the most important areas of your body (when it comes to sitting trot in particular) are in your lower body. If they start to 'misbehave' i.e. if your legs start to 'disengage' then sitting taller becomes not only more difficult but also rather pointless.

Being able to lengthen up-wards through your upper body while simultaneously stretching downwards through your lower body is the 'icing on the cake' for sitting trot.

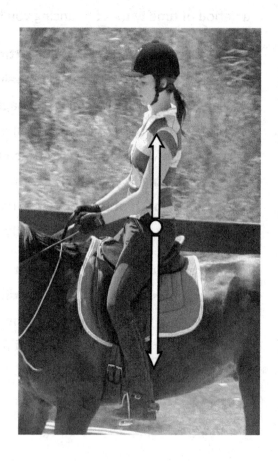

Learning to sit taller:

- In sitting trot check that your seat bones and legs are weighted correctly and that you are feeling the correct movement through your pelvis. You will need to be able maintain these prerequisites for at least half a circle to move on to this next stage.

- Breath evenly and deeply, engage your abdominal muscles and lift your sternum (where your ribs meet at the front of your chest) while keeping the back of your neck long.

- You may only get a few good strides before you feel your lower body start to 'misbehave'. You now know what to do when this starts to happen.

Your horse's movement will become softer and in turn will be easier to sit to...

...you should notice your horse start to relax when you have achieved every-thing working together. This will be a 'light bulb moment' for you and your horse.

- Even when you have worked through the previous lessons to this stage, if you feel yourself starting to stiffen, your legs starting to creep upwards etc. forget trying to lengthen through your upper body and concentrate on 're-engaging' your legs. *I cannot stress enough how important this is.*
- This 'misbehaving' happens because you are trying to achieve a difficult feat. You are asking your *lower body* to stretch downwards and to stay totally 'engaged' while at the same time you are asking your *upper body* to stretch in the opposite direction! All while sitting on a bouncing horse.
- Don't be hard on yourself if it takes a while to achieve this. It will happen, just give it time.
- When you do get a few good strides you may notice that your abdominal muscles start to ache a little (in a good way). Don't overdo it because this all requires quite a lot of muscular effort.
- You should notice your horse start to relax when you have achieved everything working together. This will be a 'light bulb moment' for you *and* your horse. Don't expect your horse to respond immediately however, it depends on how long a rider has been bouncing out of time on their back as to how long it takes a horse to relax and start to move better.
- In turn, when your horse relaxes, the trot will become softer and will become even easier to sit to.
- This is one of those upward spiral events - you ride better, your horse goes better and then you ride even better. But it has to start with you.
- Your upper body should be vertical. Any amount of leaning forward in sitting trot will cause you to bounce as your pelvis cannot move correctly when the upper body is in a forward position.
- Another tip for sitting trot is to use a wrap-around lumbar support (sold in saddlery stores). These can be invaluable for stabilising the lower back when first returning to riding or for riders with a weak lower back. They

give the rider the feeling of stronger abdominal muscles until these muscles develop through frequent riding. Some people will always need this support, most will not because riding is one of the best ways of developing stronger abdominal muscles.

Your upper body should be vertical. Any amount of leaning forward in sitting trot will cause you to bounce as your pelvis cannot move correctly when the upper body is in a forward position.

- If you feel confident enough there is a further exercise that you can do if you wish. Some find this step too challenging though. Don't attempt it if you think it is a step too far.
- Once you feel that you are able to sit tall with your upper body at the same time as you stretch down with your lower body in sitting trot, try

putting your reins in one hand and raise one arm in the air, straight up. Feel the stretch through your waist on that side. Then lower your arm, swap your reins into the other hand and raise your other arm. Then do the same on the other rein. Notice if one direction feels more difficult than the other.

Another tip for sitting trot is to use a wrap-around lumbar support (sold in saddlery stores). These can be invaluable for stabilising the lower back when first returning to riding or for riders with a weak lower back.

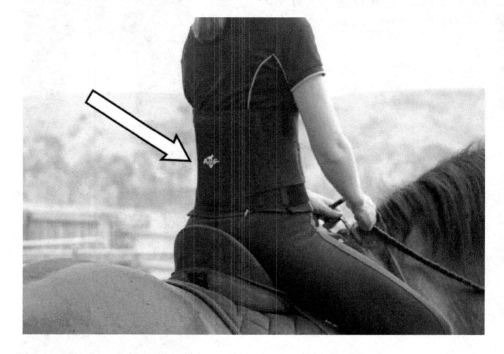

- This exercise simultaneously tests your balance *and* further improves your balance. If you manage to do this while simultaneously stretching down through your lower body you have achieved a lot.

Once you feel that you are able to sit tall with your upper body at the same time as you stretch down with your lower body in sitting trot, try putting your reins in one hand and raise one arm in the air, straight up. Feel the stretch through your waist on that side. Then lower your arm, swap your reins into the other hand and raise your other arm. Then do the same on the other rein. Notice if one direction feels more difficult than the other.

Quick summary of this lesson: In sitting trot stretch your upper body upwards as you simultaneously keep your legs 'engaged' underneath you. If you feel confident enough (and if it is safe to do so) put your reins in one hand and raise your other arm straight up in the air.

You are ready to move on to the next lesson when you can sit to the trot without bouncing for a reasonable length of time. Your horse should stay relaxed and you should not get unduly tired. You should be able to stretch up through your upper body without it affecting your lower body.

Two final lesson for the trot

These final two trotting lessons build on what you have learned so far. A rider should be able to rise on the correct diagonal by feel alone so the first lesson covers this. The second lesson consolidates everything that you have learned so far. It tests whether you really do have good timing and balance and further improves your timing, balance etc.

Final trot lesson 1: Rising straight off on the correct diagonal by feel alone

Make sure you read the Horse Rider's Mechanic website article *Rising diagonals*. Even if you do not generally ride in circles you need to work the muscles on both sides of your horse equally. You do this by changing your rising diagonal.

Now that you have mastered the three styles of trot you are ready to learn a very useful skill. Many riders never learn to do this but it is not difficult once you know how.

The skills that you now have, in particular being able to feel what your horse's back is doing (and therefore knowing what your horse's legs are doing at any point in the stride), coupled with the other skills that you have learned from the previous lessons means that you can learn to strike off on the correct diagonal in rising trot without having to look down to check.

A common way that riders check their rising diagonal is to glance (although many stare for several strides) at their horse's outside shoulder (on a circle) to see if that shoulder is going *forward* as they rise up and forward out of the saddle. If instead the outside shoulder is coming *back* as they rise they know they need to change their rising diagonal. It is possible to learn how to check by feel rather than having to look.

A common way that riders check their rising diagonal is to glance (although many stare for several strides) at their horse's outside shoulder (on a circle) to see if that shoulder is going forward as they rise up and forward out of the saddle. If instead the outside shoulder is coming back as they rise they know they need to change their rising diagonal.

Learning to rise on the correct diagonal by feel alone:

- On a left hand (anti clockwise) circle ask your horse to move up a gait from walk to trot.
- This means you are trotting on the left rein.
- (If you prefer to start on a right hand (clockwise) circle (the right rein) you will need to do the opposite to the following directions).
- Feel with your seat (pelvis) and legs (heels) for your horse's left hind (and right fore) swinging forward (remember you will feel this as a dip in your left seat bone and heel). This is when in a previous lesson you said 'left' if you had an assistant to check for you.

- Instead of saying 'left' now say 'up' and simultaneously lift your seat and let your horse's back bump you up.
- At first you may need to ride for a few strides in sitting trot saying 'up' when you feel your left seat bone dip. When you have got yourself organised you can try rising as you say 'up'.

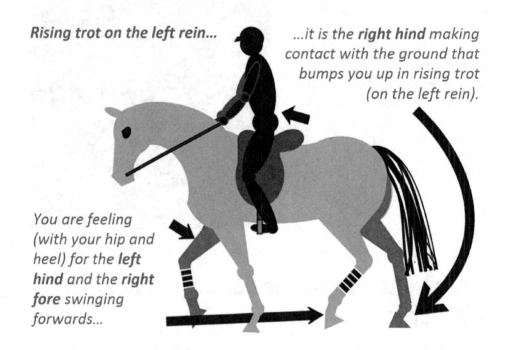

Rising trot on the left rein...

*...it is the **right hind** making contact with the ground that bumps you up in rising trot (on the left rein).*

*You are feeling (with your hip and heel) for the **left hind** and the **right fore** swinging forwards...*

- Don't forget, at the same time that your left seat bone is dipping your right seat bone is bumped upwards by your horse's right hind leg as it comes into contact with the ground. This is what actually gives you the upwards push to rise.
- It is up to you, you may feel better identifying the lifting of your outside seat bone and saying 'up' or 'rise' as you feel it lift.
- It will take a few goes before your timing becomes coordinated.
- You will find (with most horses) that they tend to push you up on the correct diagonal on one rein, almost if not every time, and push you up

on the wrong diagonal on the other rein, almost if not every time. This is because a horse is usually developed more in one set of muscles than the other (and are therefore stronger in those muscle groups). Most people are the same (unless they are virtually ambidextrous i.e. they are neither left nor right handed) and they prefer to say swing a tennis racket with one hand rather than the other (usually their right hand).

- When you are practicing this you will notice that it is much easier on one rein rather than the other to get it right . Keep changing direction until you can do it easily on both reins.

- Unless you have an assistant you may need to quickly glance at your horse's outside shoulder to check until you are confident that you are getting it right every time. Only do this though *after* you have had a go at getting it right by feel alone.

Quick summary of this lesson: In sitting trot identify when your horse's inside hind leg is swinging under the body and rise at the same time as you feel this. You may prefer to identify when the outside hind is on the ground and rise in time with that. Both will get you rising on the correct diagonal by feel alone.

You are ready to move on to the next lesson when you can rise on the correct diagonal by feel alone.

Final trot lesson 2: Alternating the three styles of trot through changes of speed, direction and gradient

You are now ready to test just how much your balance, feel and timing has improved. You should find that you are pleasantly surprised at how much better your riding has become so far. This final lesson for the trot brings together everything you have learned to this point and *further* improves your balance, feel and timing.

Learning to alternate the three styles of trot through changes of speed, direction and gradient:

- Starting off on a flat surface in a circle decide on a number, for example, four. In trot rise for four beats (on the correct diagonal), sit for four beats and then stand for four beats. Mix it up but keep alternating between the three styles of trot, aiming to change after you have counted to four.
- Switch to a larger number and practice changing between the three styles of trot, also switch to a smaller number and practice changing between the three styles of trot.
- Next practice carrying out various school movements such as figure eights etc. while changing between the three styles of trot.
- Then practice changing between the three styles of trot while asking your horse to speed up and slow down (lengthen and shorten the strides, still in trot).

- Combine changing between the three styles of trot while carrying out various school movements *and* asking your horse to speed up and slow down (lengthen and shorten the strides, still in trot).
- Once your horse's directional control and rhythm is able to be maintained, whilst also alternating between the three styles of trot, you have come a long way indeed.

Alternate the three styles of trot through changes of speed, direction and gradient. This will test your balance and will improve it further at the same time.

- If you have access to trail riding, or even if you only have access to some gradients around your arena, an excellent way of further improving your balance, feel and timing is to alternate between the three styles of trot while riding up and down various gradients.

Quick summary of this lesson: In trot decide on a number and practice changing between the three styles of trot (on the count of that number) while you change direction, speed and gradient.

You are ready to move on to the next lesson when you can change between the three styles of trot with ease and you can include changes of direction, changes of speed (lengthening and shortening of strides in trot) and changes of gradient if available.

Remember: if there is anything you do not understand or need help with after reading this book (or the others in this series) post a question on the Horse Rider's Mechanic Facebook page:

www.facebook.com/horseridersmechanic

Riding the canter

During canter your seat stays *with* the movement of your horse's back (unless you *mean* to keep your seat out of the saddle and stand up balanced in canter). This involves the pelvis *following* the circular ('loop the loop') movement of the gait.

Canter has a 'loop the loop' movement.

Canter is less 'choppy' than trot but nevertheless can be difficult to stay with until the rider has mastered the correct movement. Mastering sitting trot helps a lot with the canter as some of the skills required are very similar.

The canter can be quite fast if a horse is not balanced enough to canter slowly (a horse cannot canter slowly *while* carrying a rider until educated to do so). A further complication is that a rider is 'spun' to the outside when cantering on a circle by the centrifugal force, the less balanced the horse is, the more this occurs. So a green rider on a green horse can have quite a bit of difficulty riding this gait (one of the many reasons why 'green on green' does not usually work).

The centrifugal force

Again, when being taught to canter, most riders have usually only been told to 'sit down', 'keep your hands down' and a common one, 'relax'!

Horses vary enormously as to how comfortable they are in canter and, like trot, this is partly due to natural ability and breeding, partly due to training and partly due to the rider.

Riders should *fully master* the three styles of trot before expecting to be able to canter well however riders are often expected to canter too early. With many riders this leads to a loss of confidence (especially with riders first learning to ride or returning to riding as an adult).

The subject of jumping is not taught in this book but instructors please note that riders should never be expected to jump until they can canter well. Believe it or not it is a common occurrence to have riders jumping long before they are ready and this often leads to falls.

What should happen...

- Notice that several of the following points are the same as for sitting trot! For this reason learning to sit to the trot well will vastly improve how you ride canter (stay with me, it will make sense soon!).

- You should move *with* your horse (without bouncing), absorbing the 'loop the loop' movement of your horse's back into your lower and upper body, each area behaving differently.

- Your seat should stay with your horse through the period of suspension. This is the difficult bit, the movement of a horse's back tends to 'launch' the rider as the leading leg pushes off the ground to begin the period of suspension and the rider tends to land heavily as the diagonally opposite hind leg lands once more to begin another stride.

- Your lower body should lengthen in one direction (downwards) while your upper body lengthens in the other direction (upwards).

- Your weight should be distributed between your seat and your feet. The weight of your legs should travel down from your pelvis to your feet.

- There should be enough downwards pressure to keep adequate weight on the stirrups to keep them on your feet.

- Your upper body should be mainly upright and should give the appearance of being still while absorbing some of the movement from your horse into your lower back.

- Your hands and arms should follow the movement of your horse's head and neck.

Your lower body should lengthen in one direction (downwards) while your upper body lengthens in the other direction (upwards).

- The canter requires the correct amount of flexibility of primarily your pelvis area coupled with flexibility of the other shock absorbing joints in your legs. At the same time you need strong abdominal muscles to achieve the correct 'movement' and to stay with your horse.

In canter your horse's neck moves upwards and backwards (a) (when the legs are off the ground during the period of suspension) and forwards and down (b) (when the legs are in contact with the ground).

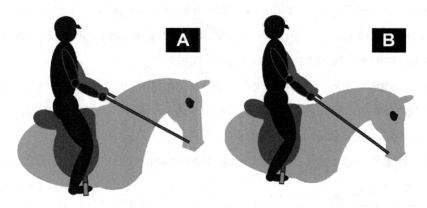

What should not happen...

- Becoming overly tired (other than what can be explained by lack of fitness).
- Upsetting your horse.
- Bouncing.
- Losing the stirrups, either partially of fully, especially the inside one on a circle.
- Pain (usually felt in the lower back area).
- Excessive leaning forwards or backwards.
- You should not *press* on the stirrups because this would push you *upwards* and would lead to bouncing as your centre of gravity would have been raised (see the **Horse Rider's Mechanic website article *Your centre of gravity***). Remember, there is a whole world of difference between allowing your weight to travel down your legs (correct) and pressing downwards through your legs (incorrect).

Losing the stirrups, either partially of fully, especially the inside one on a circle.

Canter lesson 1: Weighting your seat bones and legs correctly on a circle

The most common problem I see with riders when cantering on a circle is that they lose (or nearly lose) their inside stirrup. This occurs even with quite experienced riders and is not surprising for several reasons:

- Their horse is spinning their hips to the outside of the circle (due to the centrifugal force).
- The less balanced the horse the more this happens.
- Most riders have never been shown how to distribute their weight to counteract the effect of the centrifugal force.
- Their horse is further unbalanced by the rider 'falling to the outside' of the circle, making it even more difficult for the rider to stay balanced.
- Therefore a downward spiral of events is occurring.

This picture demonstrates the downward spiral of events that often occurs when cantering on a circle. The centrifugal force is causing the rider's hips to slide to the outside. The rider is gripping upwards with their inside leg thinking that this will help. Some riders also lean their shoulders to the inside in this case in an attempt to redress what is happening.

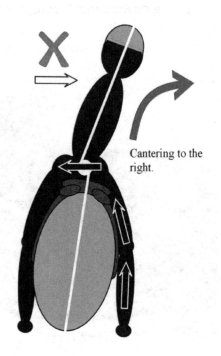

Cantering to the right.

Losing (or nearly losing) the inside stirrup is simply *the end result* of what is occurring, not the cause of it, although once a rider begins to feel insecure they usually try to grip with their legs because by now their brain is screaming at them to cling on at all costs! Unfortunately gripping with the legs simply makes the problem worse because it raises the centre of gravity even more and as you now know this is counterproductive (see the **Horse Rider's Mechanic website article** *Your centre of gravity*)

All is not lost though because there is a pretty simple solution! Even if you do not experience this problem to the degree described above, you should still work through this lesson to ensure you are weighting your seat bones and legs correctly when cantering on a circle.

Learning to weight your seat bones and legs correctly on a circle:

- Start by cantering your horse on a circle on the rein (direction) that you feel *most comfortable*. You need to practice the steps below and memorise the correct feeling so that when you change to the more problematic direction you already have the necessary tools in your toolbox.
- If this problem is particularly pronounced for you then you will benefit greatly from having an assistant.
- As you feel your hips begin to slide to the outside concentrate on *weighting* your inside stirrup. You are trying to counteract the centrifugal force. You should not *lean* to the inside but should instead aim to get more weight going down your inside leg.
- Many years ago an instructor told me 'pretend you are trying to break your inside stirrup leather'. It was a 'light bulb moment' for me and one that I have since passed on to a large number of people.

As you feel your hips begin to slide to the outside concentrate on weighting your inside stirrup. You are trying to counteract the centrifugal force (a). In time and with more education, you will both become more upright. This is helped by you first learning to distribute your weight properly so that you help rather than hinder your horse. It has to start with you. The end result should be that you have equal weight in both stirrups (b).

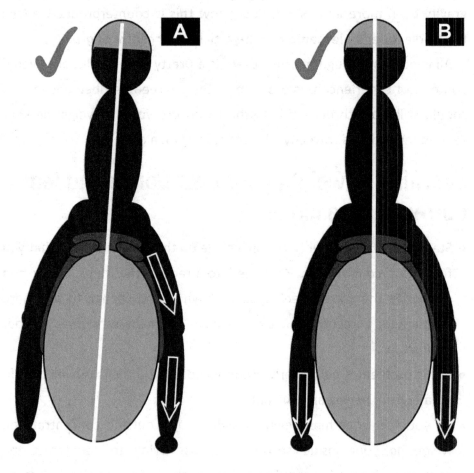

- The end result should be that you have *equal* weight in both stirrups. This is because you are already weighting the *outside* stirrup enough (due to the centrifugal force) but you have to consciously weight the inside one.

- If you have help from someone on the ground decide on a key word that your assistant can repeat out loud to you while you canter round. It could be *'inside leg, inside leg, inside leg...'* to remind you to weight your inside leg.

- By starting with weighting the legs correctly you will find that your seat bones also end up weighted correctly (for this reason it does not work to ignore your legs and concentrate on your seat bones only).

- Once you have the correct weighting going down your legs you should be able to feel your heels also moving in a 'loop the loop' movement. This is because they are now following and mirroring the ' loop the loop' movement of your horse's back in canter.

- When you are sure that you have it on your good rein switch to your 'bad rein' (make sure you give yourself and your horse a breather first. Your brain needs time to 'file' this new feeling).

- Don't aim for perfection at this stage because you will need to work through the other canter lessons to fully improve canter.

Quick summary of this lesson: In canter, start with your 'better' side on a circle and concentrate on weighting your inside leg. The faster/more unbalanced your horse the more you will have to do this. Once you have learned the correct feeling on your good rein switch to the other rein, remember the feeling and work until you have it on your 'bad' rein too.

You are ready to move on to the next lesson when you can canter on a circle in both directions without losing or nearly losing your inside stirrup and you can feel both heels following the 'loop the loop' movement of your horse's back.

Canter lesson 2: Standing in canter

Now that you have mastered *Canter lesson 1: Weighting your seat bones and legs correctly on a circle* you will have moved on a long way with any problems you may have been having with canter. This lesson will further improve your balance and your seat. You are now going to stand in the stirrups as you did in walk and trot.

Do not attempt to do this until you have fully mastered standing in the stirrups (including balancing without a neck strap) in walk and trot.

Learning to stand in canter:

- Shorten your stirrups a hole or two if necessary and use your neck strap until you are fully proficient at standing in the canter.
- If you have the space available to you it is easier to start on a straight line (such as down the long side of an arena) rather than on a circle.
- Once you feel stable enough in a straight line start to include the corners of the arena and then circles.
- In canter you will need to lean forward more than you did in trot to stay in balance.
- Start with just a few strides at a time and work up to longer.
- You will need to keep the joints in your legs (hips, knees and ankles) flexed and allow them to absorb the movement that is happening underneath you.
- You should feel as if your horse's back is like a wave and you are 'riding the wave'.
- If you find this position difficult and this difficulty is not simply due to a lack of fitness go back to *Standing trot lesson 1: Standing and staying balanced in trot* and *Standing trot lesson 2: Maintaining this position*

through changes of speed and direction and practice, practice, practice. Even if your lack of fitness is holding you back practicing standing in trot is a great way of increasing your fitness quickly.

You will need to keep the joints in your legs (hips, knees and ankles) flexed and allow them to absorb the movement that is happening underneath you...

...work up to changes of speed (within canter), direction and changes of gradient as you did for trot.

- This lesson consolidates the previous lesson. Standing balanced in your stirrups makes it difficult for you to *not* weight your inside stirrup correctly.
- For many people cantering standing can be quite challenging. Once you have mastered it, if you really want to improve your balance then you could further challenge yourself and add changes of speed (within canter), changes of direction and changes of gradient as you did for trot. Ask only for simple lead changes if you change the rein through a figure eight (i.e. come back to trot for a few strides then ask for canter on the other leading leg).

Quick summary of this lesson: In canter, starting on a straight line, stand in your stirrups and 'absorb' the movement into your hips, knees and ankles. Work up to cantering a circle on both reins, eventually without the neck strap. If, and only if, you feel confident enough add changes of speed, direction and gradient.

You are ready to move on to the next lesson when you can canter a circle (on both reins), standing and balancing in the stirrups, without holding the neck strap, absorbing the movement of your horse into your hips, knees and ankles.

Canter lesson 3: Following the movement of your horse's back

Being able to canter without bouncing is usually on the wish list of most riders after being able to sit to the trot. Many riders find it easier to canter than to sit to the trot but many bounce more than they should and this is not pleasant for them or their horse. If you have worked through the lessons to this point you now have the tools to improve your canter.

Learning to follow the movement of your horse's back:

- Starting on the rein that you usually find easiest, ask your horse to canter, making sure that you absorb the movement as your horse 'jumps' forward into canter. Many riders 'get left behind' at the moment that their horse changes from trot to canter as they lose their balance. This sometimes results in the horse getting a pull in the mouth right at the moment that they are going forward (therefore the horse is getting a go forward aid *and* a slow down aid at the same time) and this results in a frustrated horse.

- Once you have established canter, preferably in a straight line to start with, check that you have enough weight going down into your feet, feel for the dipping of both heels *at the same time* as you 'ride the waves'. Let your pelvis follow the movement, don't try to push your seat into the saddle because this will only result in you starting to bounce.

- Even though canter is a different movement to trot if you have mastered sitting trot you can use these tools to follow the movement in canter.

- It is all about keeping your legs 'engaged'. As soon as they start to 'disengage' you will start to bounce, therefore concentrate on the feeling in your feet.

- If you feel your legs starting to 'disengage' go to standing canter and then think 'kneel down' (as you did in walk and trot) and lower your seat into the saddle as you put your shoulders back. You need to put your shoulders back because in standing canter you need to lean forward for balance whereas when you sit down to canter you need to bring your shoulders back over your hips so that your pelvis can follow the movement.

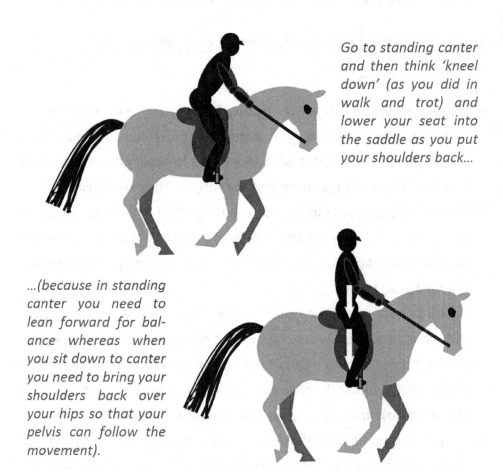

Go to standing canter and then think 'kneel down' (as you did in walk and trot) and lower your seat into the saddle as you put your shoulders back...

...(because in standing canter you need to lean forward for balance whereas when you sit down to canter you need to bring your shoulders back over your hips so that your pelvis can follow the movement).

If you still cannot get your seat to stay with your horse's back try the following:

- You need to be able to feel for the movement that is happening underneath you and let your seat follow that movement. Don't try to force your seat to stick to the saddle, this is counterproductive.
- If your legs stay 'engaged' they will 'pull you down'. Therefore you must keep your legs 'engaged'. If you start to bounce go back to standing again and so on.
- Once you think you have it, start to circle and work on getting the same feeling while also working to control the centrifugal force.

Quick summary of this lesson: In canter think about letting your weight travel down through your legs, this will keep your legs 'engaged'. If you still cannot stay with your horse try going from standing canter to sitting by lowering your seat ('kneeling down') and this will keep your legs 'engaged'.

You are ready to move on to the next lesson when you can stay with the movement of your horse in canter, initially in a straight line and eventually on a circle.

Canter lesson 4: Sitting tall and testing your balance

This final lesson for canter *tests* your balance in canter but at the same time it is the 'icing on the cake' because it further improves your balance and teaches you how to sit tall through your upper body at the same time as you stretch down through your lower body. Therefore it is similar to **Sitting trot lesson 3: Sitting taller**. Similarly it is also very good for improving any differences between the two sides of your body.

Just as for this lesson in sitting trot though, some riders find this step too challenging. Don't attempt it if you think it is a step too far.

Learning to sit tall and test your balance:

- In canter check that your seat bones and legs are weighted correctly and that you are following the movement correctly.
- Breath evenly and deeply, engage your abdominal muscles and lift your sternum (where your ribs meet at the front of your chest) while keeping the back of your neck long.
- You will probably only get a few good strides before you feel your lower body start to 'misbehave'. You know what to do when this starts to happen.
- Even when you have worked through the previous lessons to this stage, if you feel yourself starting to stiffen, your legs starting to creep upwards etc. forget trying to lengthen your upper body and concentrate on 'engaging' your legs again. *I cannot stress enough how important this is.*
- This 'misbehaving' happens because you are trying to achieve a difficult feat. You are asking your *lower body* to stretch downwards and to stay totally 'engaged' while at the same time you are asking your *upper body* to stretch in the opposite direction!

- Don't be hard on yourself if it takes a while to achieve it. It will happen, just give it time.
- This is one of those upward spiral effects, you ride better, your horse goes better and then you ride even better. But it has to start with you.

Sitting tall in canter involves stretching your upper body in the opposite direction to your lower body.

- If you feel confident enough there are two further exercises that you can do if you wish.
- To improve the engagement of your inside leg on a circle while at the same time sitting tall, put both reins in your inside hand and with your outside hand reach back to touch the back of your saddle. This exercise also helps you to feel and move correctly with the rolling action of the horse's back in canter.

- To increase the stretch through your upper body put both reins in one hand and raise one arm in the air, straight up. Feel the stretch through your waist on that side. Then lower your arm, swap your reins into the other hand and raise your other arm. Notice if one side feels more difficult than the other.

- This exercise simultaneously tests your balance *and* further improves your balance. If you manage to do this at the same time as stretching down through your lower body you have achieved a lot.

To improve the engagement of your inside leg on a circle while at the same time sitting tall, put both reins in your inside hand and with your outside hand reach back to touch the back of your saddle. This exercise also helps you to feel and move correctly with the rolling action of the horse's back in canter.

To increase the stretch through your upper body put both reins in one hand and raise one arm in the air, straight up. Feel the stretch through your waist on that side. Then lower your arm, swap your reins into the other hand and raise your other arm. Notice if one side feels more difficult than the other.

Quick summary of this lesson: In canter stretch up through your sternum and sit taller while simultaneously stretching down through your legs, keeping your lower legs in particular engaged.

Then, if you feel confident enough, put your reins in the inside hand and reach behind you with your outside hand to touch the back of the saddle. Change the rein and do the same on the other rein.

Finally, again put your reins in one hand and stretch your arm straight up in the air. Change to the other arm, then change the rein and repeat.

You have finished this lesson when you can canter on either rein without bouncing (staying with the movement of your horse). If you can also carry out the two additional stretching exercises this is a bonus.

Further reading - A list of our books

Buying a Horse Property

Buying a horse property is probably the most expensive and important purchase you will ever make. Therefore, it is very important that you get it right. There are many factors to consider and there may be compromises that have to be made. This guide to buying a horse property will help you to make many of those very important decisions.

Decisions include factors such as whether to buy developed or undeveloped land? Whether to buy a smaller property nearer the city or a larger property in a rural area? Other factors that you need to think about include the size and layout of the property, the pastures and soil, access to riding areas, the water supply, and any possible future proposals for the area. These subjects and many more are covered in this book.

A useful checklist is also provided so that you can ask the right questions before making this very important decision.

If you are buying a horse property, you cannot afford to miss out on the invaluable information in this book!

The Equicentral System Series Book 1: Horse Ownership Responsible Sustainable Ethical

With horse ownership comes great responsibility; we have a responsibility to manage our horses to the best of our ability and to do this sustainably and ethically.

Horse keeping has changed dramatically in the last 30 to 40 years and there are many new challenges facing contemporary horse owners. The modern domestic horse is now much more likely to be kept for leisure purposes than for work and this can have huge implications on the health and well-being of our horses and create heavy demands on our time and resources.

We need to rethink how we keep horses today rather than carry on doing things traditionally simply because that is 'how it has always been done'. We need to look at how we can develop practices that ensure that their needs are met, without compromising their welfare, the environment and our own lifestyle.

This book brings together much of the current research and thinking on responsible, sustainable, ethical horsekeeping so that you can make informed choices when it comes to your own horse management practices. It starts by looking at the way we traditionally keep horses and how this has come about. It then discusses some contemporary issues and offers some solutions in particular a system of horsekeeping that we have developed and call **The Equicentral System.**

For many years now we have been teaching this management system to horse owners in various climates around the world, to great effect. This system has many advantages for the 'lifestyle' of your horse/s, your own lifestyle and for the wider environment - all at the same time, a true win-win situation all round.

The Equicentral System Series Book 2: Healthy Land, Healthy Pasture, Healthy Horses

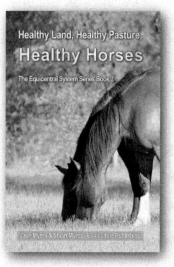

If you watch horses grazing pasture, you would think that they were made for each other. You would in fact be correct; millions of years of evolution have created a symbiotic relationship between equines (and other grazing animals) and grasslands. Our aim as horse owners and as custodians of the land should be to replicate that relationship on our land as closely as possible.

In an ideal world, most horse owners would like to have healthy nutritious pastures on which to graze their horses all year round. Unfortunately, the reality for many horse owners is far from ideal. However, armed with a little knowledge it is usually possible to make a few simple changes in your management system to create an environment which produces healthy, horse friendly pasture, which in turn leads to healthy 'happy' horses.

Correct management of manure, water and vegetation on a horse property is also essential to the well-being of your family, your animals, your property and the wider environment.

This book will help to convince you that good land management is worthwhile on many levels and yields many rewards. You will learn how to manage your land in a way that will save you time and money, keep your horses healthy and content *and* be good for the environment all at the same time. It is one of those rare win-win situations.

The Equicentral System Series Book 3: Horse Property Planning and Development

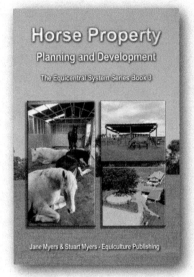

It does not matter if you are buying an established horse property, starting with a blank canvas or modifying a property you already own; a little forward planning can ensure that your dream becomes your property. Design plays a very important role in all our lives. Good design leads to better living and working spaces and it is therefore very important that we look at our property as a whole with a view to creating a design that will work for our chosen lifestyle, our chosen horse pursuit, keep our horses healthy and happy, enhance the environment and to be pleasing to the eye, all at the same time.

Building horse facilities is an expensive operation. Therefore, planning what you are going to have built, or build yourself is an important first step. Time spent in the planning stage will help to save time and money later on.

The correct positioning of fences, laneways, buildings, yards and other horse facilities is essential for the successful operation and management of a horse property and can have great benefits for the environment. If it is well planned, the property will be a safer, more productive, more enjoyable place to work and spend time with horses. At the same time, it will be labour saving and cost effective due to improved efficiency, as well as more aesthetically pleasing, therefore it will be a more valuable piece of real estate. If the property is also a commercial enterprise, then a well-planned property will be a boon to your business. This book will help you make decisions about what you need, and where you need it; it could save you thousands.

Horse Properties - A Management Guide

This book is an overview of how you can successfully manage a horse property - sustainably and efficiently. It also complements our one day workshop - *Healthy Land, Healthy Pasture, Healthy Horses*.

This book offers many practical solutions for common problems that occur when managing a horse property. It also includes the management system that we have designed, called - **The Equicentral System**.

This book is a great introduction to the subject of land management for horsekeepers. It is packed with pictures and explanations that help you to learn, and will make you want to learn even more.

Some of the subjects included in this book are:
The grazing behaviour of horses.
The paddock behaviour of horses.
The dunging behaviour of horses.
Integrating horses into a herd.
Land degradation problems.
The many benefits of pasture plants.
Horses and biodiversity.
Grasses for horses.
Simple solutions for bare soil.
Grazing and pasture management.
Grazing systems.
Condition scoring.
Manure management... and much more!

A Horse is a Horse - of Course

Understanding horse behaviour is a very important part of caring for horses. It is very easy to convince yourself that your horse is content to do all of the things that you enjoy, but a better approach is to understand that your horse sees the world quite differently to you, after all, you are a primate (hunter/gatherer) and your horse is a very large hairy herbivore! So it's not surprising that you both have a very different view of the world.

A good approach is to take everything 'back to basics' and think about what a horse has evolved to be. This book describes horse behaviour in both the wild 'natural' environment and in the domestic environment. It then looks at how you can reduce stress in the domestic horse by understanding and acknowledging their real needs, resulting in a more 'well-adjusted', content and thriving animal.

Do your horse a favour and read this book!

Horse Rider's Mechanic Workbook 1: Your Position

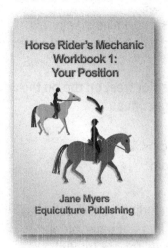

Horse Rider's Mechanic
Workbook 1:
Your Position

Jane Myers
Equiculture Publishing

Many common horse riding problems, including pain and discomfort when riding, can be attributed to poor rider position. Often riders are not even aware of what is happening to various parts of their body when they are riding. Improving your position is the key to improving your riding. It is of key importance because without addressing the fundamental issues, you cannot obtain an 'independent seat'.

This book looks at each part of your body in great detail, starting with your feet and working upwards through your ankles, knees and hips. It then looks at your torso, arms, hands and head. Each chapter details what each of these parts of your body should be doing and what you can do to fix any problems you have with them. It is a step by step guide which allows you to fix your own position problems.

After reading this book, you will have a greater understanding of what is happening to the various parts of your body when you ride and why. You will then be able to continue to improve your position, your seat and your riding in general. This book also provides instructors, riding coaches and trainers with lots of valuable rider position tips for teaching clients. You cannot afford to miss out on this great opportunity to learn!

Horse Rider's Mechanic Workbook 2: Your Balance

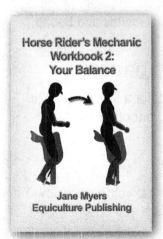

Horse Rider's Mechanic
Workbook 2:
Your Balance

Jane Myers
Equiculture Publishing

Without good balance, you cannot ride to the best of your ability. After improving your position (the subject of the first book in this series), improving your balance will lead to you becoming a more secure and therefore confident rider. Improving your balance is the key to *further* improving your riding. Most riders need help with this area of their riding life, yet it is not a commonly taught subject.

This book contains several lessons for each of the three paces, walk, trot and canter. It builds on *Horse Rider's Mechanic Workbook 1: Your Position*, teaching you how to implement your now improved position and become a safer and more secure rider. The lessons allow you to improve at your own pace, in your own time. They will compliment any instruction you are currently receiving because they concentrate on issues that are generally not covered by most instructors.

This book also provides instructors, riding coaches and trainers with lots of valuable tips for teaching clients how to improve their balance. You cannot afford to miss out on this great opportunity to learn!

You can read the beginning of each of these books (for free) on the on the Equiculture website www.equiculture.com.au

We also have a website just for Horse Riders Mechanic www.horseridersmechanic.com

All of our books are available in various formats including paperback, as a PDF download and as a Kindle ebook. You can find out more on our websites where we offer fantastic package deals for our books!

Make sure you sign up for our mailing list while you are on our websites so that you find out when they are published. You will also be able to find out about our workshops and clinics while on the websites.

Recommended websites and books

Our websites www.equiculture.com.au and www.horseridersmechanic.com have links to our various Facebook pages and groups. They also contain extensive information about horsekeeping, horse care and welfare, riding and training, including links to other informative websites and books.

Bibliography of scientific papers

Please go to our website www.equiculture.com.au for a list of scientific publications that were used for this book and our other books.

Final thoughts

Thank you for reading this book. We sincerely hope that you have enjoyed it. Please consider leaving a review of this book at the place you bought it from, or contacting us with feedback, stuart@equiculture.com.au, so that others may benefit from your reading experience.

CPSIA information can be obtained
at www.ICGtesting.com
Printed in the USA
FSOW04n0441151216
28566FS